CLEARED FOR TAKEOFF

THE RUNWAY TO EFFECTIVE LEADERSHIP

CLEARED FOR TAKEOFF

THE RUNWAY TO EFFECTIVE LEADERSHIP

Todd Michael Herrington

VMH™ Publishing
3355 Lenox Rd. NE Ste 750
Atlanta, GA 30326
vmhpublishing.com

LCCN: 2021907369

Hardback ISBN: 978-1-947928-92-3

Paperback: 978-1-947928-78-7

EBook: 978-1-947928-83-1

Book Designed by Vikki Jones

Published in United States of America

10 9 8 7 6 5 4 3 2 1

Dedicated to the Spirit of Delta and the employees who came together to become more than a team but a family who fought and struggled their way to the top of an industry.

Special thanks to all those who trusted enough in me to hire me and then continued to put their trust in me, despite my frequent failures.

CONTENTS

PREFACE

My mother used to marvel at how good fortune always seemed to come my way. Growing up, even though I never really charted out a course to reach my goals, things always seemed to work out for me. Take finding a summer job in high school or internships in college. After several timely opportunities fell right into my lap, some family friends came up with a saying about me: "Todd always lands jelly-side up." It's something that's stuck with me throughout my life and career. (In reality, I know that my "jelly-side up" tendencies happen because God takes care of me, and I've almost always just allowed that to happen without worrying too much about the bad things that happen in between.)

I don't mean to imply that I didn't help to make my own luck during my career. I forged a lot of relationships that ended up creating some of those opportunities that came my way. In many ways, though, I've mastered the art of being in the right spot at the right time. However, timing is something that you can't always control.

Perhaps the best combination of good fortune and timing that came my way was getting an opportunity to work for one of the greatest companies ever founded. For nearly 20 years, I was lucky enough to be a part of the tight-knit family called Delta Air Lines.

What most people I worked with over that time don't know about me is that I only ended up at this Fortune 500 company because I had failed as an entrepreneur. While finishing up my bachelor's degree in Mechanical Engineering at Georgia Tech, my best friend Steve and I went into business together. We planned to take over the world by designing and building home theaters and home automation systems. After we graduated, with a business bank loan in hand and a cash loan from my parents to put food on the table for a few months, I was off and running toward that vision!

What I hadn't quite calculated correctly was the value that I was bringing to the partnership. Or, in this case, the value I *wasn't* bringing. Steve was an expert in everything related to home electronics. In high school and all throughout college, he had worked part-time or full-time in consumer electronics stores or mom-and-pop home theater design and installation companies. He had an avid interest in keeping up with all of the latest technology, AV equipment, hardware, and software in the electronics industry. He knew how to piece it all together into systems he could sell to almost anyone who had more cash than ideas about what to do with it. Everything he did in business was centered around his passion for electronics, which made him extremely good at it.

By contrast, I had no background in any of that stuff other than the fact that I enjoyed having access to the cool equipment he brought back from his store. As Steve's roommate in college,

I loved being the only guys we knew who had a 7.2-channel surround sound system with a 120-inch projection screen in our little Dunwoody apartment. But I really wasn't bringing anything to the table other than enthusiasm for the idea of making a lot of money and co-owning a business. I made the mistake of not caring what kind of business I co-owned. I just liked the idea of being a boss and, hopefully, a successful entrepreneur. I never asked myself what I would actually be contributing to the team.

Not surprisingly, a few months after graduation, Steve and I figured out that the partnership wasn't working. As the majority partner, he made a decision that, as my friend, I'm sure was devastating for him to have had to make—he had to let me go. Though both of us knew he was right to do it, I still wasn't thrilled about it. It took us a few years to reconnect. (Steve did really well growing his business, subsequently. He pursued what he loved and, as a result, he was able to reach all of the goals he set out to achieve. He's also godfather to my youngest daughter, Sylvia, and I am honored that his middle daughter, Emily, is my goddaughter.)

Being fired is never fun, but looking back on it, it was the best thing that could have happened to me at the time. Aside from the short-term depression that you go through when you are terminated from a job, what ultimately happens is that you realize that it's not the end of the world. In fact, it can free you of the thing people fear the most—the fear of the unknowns associated with it. This basic fear holds many people back from sharing what they feel is right or standing their ground when they have good ideas that need to be implemented. Instead, they often wait for others around them to be the first to take a stand, and this is the first step to getting passed over for leadership opportunities. The people who quickly learn to let go of their fear of the unknown and of being without a job are the ones who, time and time again, get recognized by their peers and superiors alike as the best candidates to lead people. I credit this experience, before I went into my first job in corporate America, for helping me overcome that fear.

On the same day that I was let go from my position as chief technology officer[1] of Synergy Multimedia, LLC, I had dinner with a classmate of mine from Tech. Having been an intern there for several semesters while he was in school, he had a lot of contacts within the Engineering Department at the jet base. He offered to keep an ear to the ground for any openings for engineers.

It was only seven months after the tragedy of the 9/11 terror attacks, so the airline industry was in disarray and not exactly in a hiring mode. September 11th was the straw that broke the backs of the airlines, marking the beginning of a great recession for many industries. It would take years for the economy to feel like it was really moving again. I thanked Jesse for offering to look out for something, but I really didn't expect any follow-up.

To my surprise, I woke up the next day to a call from Jesse asking if I would like to be considered for a contract engineering opportunity that was opening up in Delta's composite repair shop. He had just been contacted by his old boss, Bill Visage,

[1] I know, very lofty title for a 22-year-old kid with just a couple of college internships under his belt.

who needed to bring someone in quickly for a repair project. Cost-saving projects were the only thing still in vogue at the Delta hangar, and Bill was up to his elbows in too many of them. In fact, he was so overworked that he didn't have time to go out recruiting and interviewing a bunch of contract engineering candidates. So, he made a few calls to his former interns, trusting that one of them would recommend someone to him who would be at least halfway competent. Luckily for me, Jesse was the first person Bill had called. Even luckier, Jesse thought I fell into the "at least halfway competent" bucket.

Not knowing what the word "composite" really meant, I eagerly gave Bill a call about the job opportunity and told him I was interested in coming in to take a look at the project. Apparently, it was only five minutes after Bill had hung up the phone on Jesse when I called him back. Years later, Bill told me that because I had responded so quickly, he didn't even bother to keep looking for candidates. A little put off by management asking him to play Human Resources, he had taken it as good fortune that he had a candidate in hand after less than five minutes of due diligence. Apparently, he had wheeled back his chair and turned to one of his fellow office mates, Nathan Schulz[2], and asked, "Jesse wouldn't recommend someone he didn't trust, right?"

---

2 Nathan would later become my technical mentor. I learned more about how to be a detail-oriented engineer from him than anyone I've ever worked with. He taught me everything I know about structural analysis of aircraft repairs. The guys on the shop floor, like Gerald Sakala, Rodney Brown, and Kent Berner taught me the rest of what I needed to know – everything from how to use a bucking bar to properly designing tools that worked.

After a brief on-site interview the next day, and a month-long series of background checks, fingerprinting, and other required corporate pre-hire checkpoints, I had a job. I didn't know it at the time, but I was about to be a part of one of the wildest rides in commercial airline history! How's that for landing jelly-side up?

In the early 2000s, all the big commercial passenger carriers (United, American, Delta, Northwest, US Airways, and Continental) were still operating with a pre-deregulation mindset, as though they were back in the days when the government had controlled fares, routes, and the market entry of new airlines. They hadn't adjusted to a free-market environment yet. Delta was no different. We were saddled with bad aircraft deals[3] and fuel prices that were higher than our business model had been built for, we were regionally focused where we should have been thinking internationally, and our model didn't value the business traveler as much as it should have. The company lacked a lot of the clear vision and leadership that would arise later in the decade—the type of vision and leadership that would usher the entire airline industry into a golden age unlike anything seen in the inaugural century of passenger flight.

Delta had also lost its way by moving away from a core group of airline people leading the company: bankers and other outsiders were leading us at that time. Delta's CEO, Leo Mullin (a former banker), had brought in a whole team of people from other industries to run the complicated airline

3 The 20-year exclusive deal with Boeing was supposed to give Delta the most favored pricing in the world (according to Boeing). Unfortunately, it precluded any benefits that competition would have brought.

business. Now, there's nothing wrong with bankers and outsiders. They can bring a fresh look to an aged company. Ed Bastian, Delta's current CEO, has a banking background, for example. But what makes Ed Bastian different from Leo Mullin is that Ed spent a significant amount of time in the airline industry before becoming CEO of Delta Air Lines. He is, principally, an airline person. More importantly, Ed was a *Delta* person. Leo Mullin, according to many of the old guard at Delta, was anything but.

It certainly isn't impossible for someone to come into an industry from the outside, then provide phenomenal leadership and bring about success. However, in a large, complicated business sector like commercial aviation, it is extremely difficult to be effective when you don't surround yourself with people who have a deep understanding of what makes that type of business run effectively at every level. All of us who were around Delta to see the difference between Leo Mullin and his immediate successors (especially Jerry Grinstein and Richard Anderson) were able to draw several conclusions about leadership and the real difference that strong leaders can make to a company.

Having the luxury of having been part of Delta's journey from being a poorly managed, lumbering, overgrown regional airline in the early post-9/11 era to a company willing to fight hard during the tough time when we entered into bankruptcy, and then on to being a formidable worldwide competitor and industry leader post-bankruptcy, I had a crash course in Business Leadership 101 (and probably 102, as well). The company made its share of mistakes, but fortunately the good decisions far outweighed the bad ones.

As a result of fantastic leadership at Delta's helm over the past 15 years, thousands of us who stuck it out during the tough times and fought the good fight learned how to assimilate and imitate the model that was put in place for us, and we became effective leaders ourselves. We were given huge opportunities to grow, not only in our business and in our personal pocketbooks, but also as people who had a clear set of common core principles. These principals were so simple that all of us could adopt them and make decisions easily, even without a lot of specific guidance from Human Resources or executive management. Our CEO re-reestablished the old business principles that had been set in place by our founder, Collett Everman (C.E.) Woolman, who set Delta's culture way back in the first half of the twentieth century. In fact, the principles established by Woolman are so integral to Delta's leadership style that I begin each chapter with a quotation from him related to the chapter's topic. They really are timeless and are core to the eternal Spirit of Delta.

The leadership model at Delta during that golden age of commercial aviation spread like wildfire across several thousand lower-level managers and supervisors. The result was the creation of many millionaires across all ranks within the company, from the mechanics in the hangar to the frontline team members working in Operational Control Center across the runway. As I write this book, even though we are still in the midst of a crippling global pandemic which has largely paralyzed our industry, over 17,000 of my colleagues at Delta have made the decision that they were financially comfortable enough to take a voluntary separation package to help ensure Delta would carry on and continue to be a dominant player in the airline industry for years to come. Many of the thousands who have elected to leave are capable of retiring without worrying about running out of money for the rest of their lives. This amazing feat was made possible because of the way the leadership team at Delta led the company and the rewards that came in for all of us as a result, which I will elaborate on in Chapter 9.

Although I will continue to seek some type of employment for at least another few years, I'm one of the 17,000-plus Delta employees who were fortunate enough to be able to say that I could pursue almost any business endeavor I wanted to without the fear of failure or worries about what I'll put on the table for my family for the foreseeable future. This financial freedom is largely due to the successes we had as a team due to the amazing leadership we had in place at Delta.

As I retire from commercial aviation, I'm writing this book to pass on some of the gems I picked up during my time at Delta. Each chapter that follows covers a different aspect of leadership, from having and communicating your vision to developing goals and a plan, then letting the plan fail in order to succeed. We tried a lot of things that didn't work. But, we also did a lot of things that worked really well. For anyone who wants the secrets of success that we discovered during the greatest era of commercial aviation, I'll tell you everything I've learned. And here's a spoiler: it's all about how you lead people!

This book reflects the opinions and experience of the author only and is not endorsed or otherwise approved by Delta.

INTRODUCTION

At certain moments in the history of every organization, there are major inflections points. Some are so extreme that they threaten the very core of the organization, meaning that one false move at the top could end in the total failure of the entire enterprise. At Delta Air Lines, we went through one of those points nearly 20 years ago, and we lived on the edge of a knife for about half a decade. For years, we all came to work wondering how long we could sustain losing millions of dollars each day we continued operating aircraft, which, of course, was every day of the year. None of us could have known what lay in wait ahead of us on our journey, but we would be forever changed, both as a company and as individuals, by the timely arrival of a new team of leaders who came on board in the mid-2000s.

When I arrived at the jet base in Atlanta in the summer of 2002, times were rough for airlines. All of the carriers in the US were looking to cut costs however they could. We were all reeling from bad business models that were crumbling beneath us. The post-9/11 world, where planes were less than half full most of the time, only accelerated our daily losses.

An iconic symbol of our storied maintenance hangar was a big, reddish-orange neon sign on top of one of the roofing truss structures that broadcast the message "Fly Delta Jets" in the hours of darkness on the approach to the Atlanta International Airport. The first time I ever flew into Atlanta, it was in the wee hours of the morning, and I remember seeing that big neon sign as we landed. For me, that was a major part of the airline's branding—the thing that really stuck in my mind when I thought about Delta Air Lines. It was a symbol of our headquarters and a beacon to all those passing through the capital of the southeastern United States—Atlanta, Georgia.

We shut off the lights to that sign shortly after the attacks on the World Trade Center, to save on our electric bill. It was a sad moment for many who called Atlanta home. As a sign of the times, it felt like everything was going into a state of hibernation. It was as if the hangar building itself was going to sleep and waiting for better times. We stopped buying pens, pencils, notebooks, and erasers. We even stopped the delivery of the replacement water tanks to our water coolers. Every nonessential job was eliminated, and the bean counters in Finance were running out of beans to count. Like General Washington's army at Valley Forge, we had no supplies, and we were hunkering down for a long winter. It was a funny time to get *into* commercial aviation. Everyone else I met there seemed to be building a plan to get *out* of it.

I watched as my colleagues turned their coats and ran away from aviation. When I arrived at Delta in 2002, an assortment of 22 engineers worked in the mezzanine office I was assigned to. A year later, only four of us remained. I was never happy to see anybody go, but as a contractor looking to get on direct, it did become easier to officially become a member of the family with each engineer who decided to leave. (I finally made progress in December of 2003, when I replaced a young lady named Jessica, who decided to try her luck in law school up in New York. It was the last direct engineering position that Delta Air Lines offered for nearly two years. Lucky timing!)

Even those way at the top were bailing out and pulling open their golden parachutes. At least they had millions of dollars in severance plans to fall back on. Those of us who chose to stay enjoyed a double-barrel-full of pay *cuts*. One came in 2004 and another right around the corner in 2005—the same year that we filed for Chapter 11 federal bankruptcy restructuring protection.

Our knight in shining armor was a man by the name of Gerald "Jerry" Grinstein. Jerry came on as CEO at Delta in 2004 after the previous regime of bankers and outsiders had left the company. He was a railroad and airline guy. He had been CEO of Western Airlines in the mid-1980s when they merged with Delta. That was back when Delta had been strictly a southeastern regional airline. The merger with Western was the beginning of Delta becoming a major transcontinental carrier. When Jerry Grinstein came back on board with us, we were in debt by a staggering $23.8 billion. We were financially broke.

At a time when airline executives were awarding themselves handsome, multimillion-dollar annual salaries, Jerry Grinstein agreed to come on board for $450,000 per year with no stock options (which would have been worthless, anyway), and he went without any bonuses. When he had to make the difficult decision to slash our salaries by another 10 percent (the second round of pay cuts mentioned above), he reduced his own salary to $325,000 per year. That fact did not go unnoticed by any of us. Also, the pilot's union, ALPA, had been at odds with the previous CEO's team over the gratuitous salaries and bonuses that they took while asking ALPA to slash the pilots' pay. Before Jerry came in, the pilots had been threatening to strike. Jerry was able to diffuse tensions with the union and avoid strikes as he re-established trust, which also didn't go unnoticed.

Jerry became something of a folk hero to all of us on the front line. He was signing up for the same hits we were taking. He was also personable; he walked the hangar floor and got to know some of the guys in the maintenance bays and out on the ramp. None of the folks I ever worked with remembered Leo Mullin ever doing the same. It's not to say that he hadn't ever walked the floor. But the fact that none of the people I worked with remember him doing it says something. At a time when all of us needed to know someone was with us, we could put a face on a leader who was standing with us, fighting for our survival.

Jerry was walking through the hangar one day when he ran into one of my friends, Al Koller. Al was one of the mechanics I worked with in the hangar composite repair shop, and he was about to reach his 40-year work anniversary with Delta. He was an old Pan Am guy from New York who had come to Delta after Pan Am collapsed in the early 1990s. Jerry came up to him and started to chat with him, and Al mentioned that his anniversary was coming up soon. As Jerry was leaving, Al said, in his thick New York accent, "Hey Jerry, you gonna come to my 40th pin ceremony, or what?" Jerry had never met Al before that day, but he gave him a smile and promised to come. Al smiled back, and his buddies in the shop teased him about it after Jerry had left and for several weeks afterward. Nobody thought Jerry would actually show up. But he did. And he was the one that presented Al with his anniversary pin, himself. Al's buttons nearly popped off his shirt. All the guys in Hangar Bay 5 remembered that for a long time.

For the first time in years, we had a CEO who was one of us. He was a bona fide member of the Delta family, and we all adored him. Even the pilots managed to like him. The guy was all-in for us and believed in the Delta Spirit. He didn't *need* to be there with us—he could easily have retired years earlier—but he had *chosen* to be there, and we appreciated it. Jerry worked his tail off for us, and, more importantly, he used two of his strongest leaders, Ed Bastian (the CFO) and Jim Whitehurst (the COO), to do one of the most brilliant restructuring jobs of any major US corporation in any industry.

Jerry knew he needed to rely on and trust his frontline people, but he also knew enough to trust his closest inner circle and allow them to effectively restructure and run the airline. And those two, Ed Bastian and Jim Whitehurst, were smart enough to bring in outside help to get us trained with the right skills and reset our mindset to come out of our long winter of bankruptcy with the confidence to start to win the war of survival and (amazingly) to make money again.

There was an exact moment when we all knew we were going to make it and be okay. Late in 2006, US Airways CEO,

Doug Parker[4], put in a bid for a hostile takeover of Delta. His bid was for around $10 billion, at a time where many of our creditors valued us a lot lower. Some thought we were only worth around $6 billion coming out of bankruptcy, so a lot of serious thought went into accepting this takeover bid.

Doug Parker wanted to move Delta's corporate office to Arizona. This was the corporate office location for America West Airlines, who ended up buying US Airways in 2005. Doug had arranged that merger too, so this was going to be a continuation of his consolidated airline empire. Naturally, we all hated this idea.

We were an Atlanta company, one with southern roots going back to our foundation. "Corporate office relocation to Arizona? For Delta? You've got to be kidding!" It wasn't only the employees who hated this idea. Atlanta's mayor, Georgia's congressional representatives, and US senators were all strongly opposed to it. Jerry, Ed, and Jim remained calm and fought a brilliant campaign on all our behalf.

A simple grass-roots slogan was coined: "*Keep Delta My Delta*!" We had buttons, T-shirts, lanyards, key chains—you name it—made. We petitioned our state capital, the US Congress, the president, our passengers—anyone who would listen—that it would be a bad idea to let this takeover happen. Jerry, Ed, and Jim quietly encouraged all of it and kept right on working on our bankruptcy emergence plan. They also lobbied our creditors, ultimately convincing them that a Delta Air Lines emerging from bankruptcy alone would be a much

---

4 Doug Parker later became CEO of American Airlines when US Airways merged with American during American's bout with bankruptcy in 2012.

more powerful, profitable airline than one married to an ugly bride like US Airways.

Our networks didn't marry up well, our cultures weren't a good match (not that US Airways had any distinct culture at all), and it wouldn't add any value for our passengers, as many of our routes would be duplicates of what they already flew, so capacity would be naturally reduced, forcing ticket prices up.

Our senior leaders came up with a better plan. They worked out an arrangement for a much more sensible merger, one where Delta would be the dominant party in the merger instead of the one being absorbed. Corporate headquarters would remain in Atlanta in the plan they started to hatch, and the route structure born of this new merger would be one of the best marriages in the history of commercial airline mergers. Apparently, our senior leaders successfully sold this plan because the broader group of creditors who held our debt rejected Doug Parker's hostile takeover bid in February 2007. Later in the same year, our future would include an amicable merger with a fellow Sky Team partner—Northwest Airlines—who was based in Minneapolis, Minnesota.

It's funny how sometimes fate aligns at a particular moment. Just as the news of the rejection of the US Airways hostile takeover was announced, Jerry, Ed, and Jim were scheduled to do something else that would really reawaken the Spirit of Delta. And the timing just couldn't have been any sweeter. The three of them made their way to the top of the Tech Ops hangar facility during the dark, evening hours in late February. With several hundred mechanics, engineers, planners, logistics personnel, pilots, flight attendants, and many other frontline employees watching (and wearing their Keep Delta My Delta paraphernalia), a countdown started.

When that countdown hit zero, Jerry, Ed, and Jim flipped a giant switch and that big, old, reddish-orange Fly Delta Jets neon sign was emblazoned across the Atlanta night sky once again. I get tears in my eyes just thinking about that moment. Grown men hugging other grown men. Crying. Cheering. All of us just absolutely in love with our company and feeling like we'd just won the war. And really, we had! That was the exact moment we knew it. And we won because we had the best damned leadership team in the airline industry. And Delta Air Lines never looked back from there. It was full throttle ahead. The runway was clear, and we were about to take off!

The hallmark of leadership, in any kind of organization, is the ability to take an idea, get people to rally around that idea, and then inspire those people to figure out a plan which will make that idea into reality. Good leadership takes good ideas and makes them happen. You don't have to be a genius to be a good leader. You don't even need to be clever. Heck, the idea you have doesn't even have to be yours because the key to being a truly great leader is to make everything the team does about them, not you.

For years now, I've had a plaque on my desk that reminds me of these principles. It reads, "There is no limit to what a man can do or where he can go if he doesn't mind who gets credit." Ronald Reagan had plaque with that motto on his desk. My grandfather had it on his desk, too. I took it when he passed away and put it on my desk to remind me that you achieve the most success when you instill into the minds of your team that the idea that you are chasing is their idea: the goals are their goals and the plan is their plan. Consequently, when the team is successful, it is their success. Who cares about the credit, so long as you can all share the reward?

Getting people to become energized about a plan is not that hard to do. You just have to know the basic principles of leadership to harness the power behind any team you have. The one promise I can give you is that if you follow the principles outlined in the chapters of this book, even if you lack genius, you'll find a way to realize your vision. And if that involves making a whole lot of money for your company, then that's great. If it means something even more fulfilling, then even better. In the end, if you do it right, you'll probably have the respect of your team as well—even if they don't tell you all the time.

CHAPTER 1

The Importance of Vision

Inspiration and, above all, vision is needed on the part of those who control the destiny of our company.
–C.E. Woolman

Over the past ten years, I've had several dozen employees approach me, expressing the desire to become a manager. I always ask these people to tell me what areas of the business they are interested in managing. Too often, they tell me that they will do anything, and they don't really care which area of the company they go to as long as the title is "manager," "general manager," "director," or something similar.

I understand the feeling of wanting to be in charge. And, yes, I do know that people, generally, give more respect to people who have these titles—whether it be right or wrong, it happens. I was shocked, for example, how some people who never used to respond to my phone calls suddenly started diligently calling me back when my title changed from "engineer" to "manager." So, I understand the desire for that title change. However, when you're shopping around for a leader to hire, the candidates who are only interested in the title of the position they are applying for raise a huge red flag. Nobody ever got inspired to work for a person whose sole vision was to take on a role because of its title.

Speaking of titles, let's talk about job titles that use the word manager. There is a distinct difference between the roles of someone who manages work and someone who is a manager of a team. A project manager, for example, manages all aspects of making sure that the tasks related to a project are planned out, responsibilities are assigned to distinct task owners, and that milestones are tracked to completion. It is their job to manage the tasks that need to be done to ensure that the project plan is executed successfully. Team leads are usually assigned to manage the day-to-day tasks and to make sure work assignments are given out to the people who can most effectively do the work.

Managers of people, however, are really *not* people who are hired to just manage work. They are hired to inspire and lead people toward a goal. You can certainly inspire people and lead in roles where you are genuinely just expected to manage the day-to-day tasks, but you don't have to be a great leader to do those roles effectively. You *cannot* be a successful manager of people if you never figure out how to inspire and lead.

As much as I appreciate people who have ambition, it is not the attribute that inspires a team. A team looks for a vision from a leader. And you can't lead people to any kind of success if you don't have a clear picture of what success would look like. Imagine if you showed up to a new job and nobody told you what they expected from you or gave you direction on what you were supposed to do. Would that make you feel motivated to do anything, let alone anything great? Some of you reading this may be champions of the 5S principles of Lean organizational management. One of the foundations of 5S is establishing what "good" is supposed to look like. Well, guess what? If you don't have a vision for the team, none of them know what "good" looks like either. If you have no vision, why are you interested in leading? And how in the world are you going to know if the team is succeeding?

For those of you out there that have the ambition to get into leadership and who feel attracted to the idea of leading people, I'm going to let you in on the secret behind the first step: you have to start with an idea of where you are taking the team. You'd never consider voting for someone for public office that didn't have a platform—someone who said, "Vote for me because I want the title of 'president.'" That would not be a winning campaign slogan. So why would you apply for a job as a leader with that mindset?

Think of the guy who's put 20-something years into the company (maybe staying in the same role throughout) who has a new manager coming into his group. What is he going to be interested in knowing from day one? Honestly, the main thing he's going to care about is where the new guy or gal is taking them (and whether or not they are going to be a pain in their posterior). If you don't have the foggiest clue what your answer to that question would be, you probably took the job for the wrong reason, and you going to start off on a bad footing with your new team. And if you were the one who hired someone into that role without asking them where they wanted to take the team, then shame on you for not asking. That should have been your first question during the interview process.

A lot of people confuse having a vision for having goals. It's okay to go into a new role without specific goals. In fact, you should probably go into any new leadership role without a firm idea of what the team's goals will be unless you are already familiar with the team, their capabilities, and what their problems are. Even if you think you know all of this, your team won't trust you if they aren't a part of the goal-setting process, so you might as well hold off on setting the goals in stone either way.

A vision is a high-level direction that you want to set for your team. It is an aspiration. It is more than an abstract idea but not necessarily something that is measurable, at least not at first. If you can measure it along the way, then it's a goal. Instead, your vision should answer this question: what do I want to do with this team when I take the reins?

For example, one of the teams I eventually managed at Delta was the 24-7 Liaison Engineering team. This is the group that gets the calls in the middle of the night when an aircraft full of passengers is getting ready to take off from Dusseldorf to Atlanta, and the maintenance crew notices that one of the overhead bins won't stay shut. The maintenance manual from Boeing or Airbus may require replacement of the broken latch. Well, if the mechanic in Dusseldorf doesn't have that latch, you're going to need Engineering to authorize a different procedure—

unless you want to cancel the 200-passenger flight while you wait for the latch to arrive on a rescue flight.

Now imagine you're in the Maintenance Control Center and you get a frantic call from Dusseldorf Line Maintenance telling you they need an alternate repair method asap. You, in turn, call the 24-7 Liaison Engineering group for help. The 20-something-year-old on the other end of the line tells you that they don't have the necessary expertise in overhead bins and that you need to get in touch with the Cabin Interiors Engineer who is the overhead bin expert. That fresh-out-of-college kid gives you a couple of names and phone numbers and wishes you luck.

Now you pick up the phone and try the first number. The call goes straight to voicemail. You try the second number. No answer. You look up the manager's name for the Cabin Engineering team and it takes him 15 minutes to wipe the sleep out of his eyes, fire up his laptop, log in, then find a picture of the damaged overhead bin that the liaison engineer had already looked at 25 minutes ago. That guy figures out a good solution, but he's a little rusty, so it takes him 30 minutes longer than someone who does this stuff every day to get you the information you need to move that airplane.

So, you just made 200 passengers wait an extra 25 minutes on the ground while you played phone tag and waited for a guy to wake up and boot up his computer. Then you waited an extra 30 minutes while this guy, who isn't used to issuing authorizations in emergency situations, fumbles around working out how to use that computer. All in all, you wasted nearly an hour because a kid on solo shift couldn't be bothered to pick up a phone and try to work through a solution directly with the cabin manager. And on top of that, that kid didn't learn anything, so the next time that situation comes up, the same 55 minutes will get wasted all over again. Worse yet, maybe the cabin guy will be on vacation next time, and by the time someone with half a clue is able to come up with a solution, the air crew will have timed out and the flight will be cancelled!

Well, in this story, that Cabin Engineering Manager was me in the summer of 2013. That type of scenario had played out more times than I cared to count in the short year and a half that I served in that role, and the Maintenance Control Center, Line Maintenance, air crews, and passengers all over the world were frequently frustrated. And I got woken up in the middle of the night a whole lot, as did my wife.

You think I had a vision for what I'd do if I ever got a chance to run that 24-7 Liaison Engineering team? You bet I did! I had three ideas right off the bat!

Vision 1: Build a knowledge base of for liaison engineers across all subject matter so that the on-site team can come up with solutions to 90% of the problems that are experienced on the line.

Vision 2: When the existing knowledge base of the team can't cover the issue at hand, *never* tell the Control Center or Line Maintenance to call another engineer. If someone else needs to be called, the Liaison Engineer calls them and learns from the expert they contacted so they know the solution the next time.

Vision 3: Be known as a reliable solution center that is a dependable, one-stop shop for solutions. Earn the respect of other teams by minimizing their loss of sleep from calls in the middle of the night. (Okay, that last one was a bit personal.)

Notice that none of those visions are particularly measurable day-to-day or month-to-month. They are aspirations. You only know if you're successful from anecdotal evidence or subjective feedback from other teams. At the same time, they're very clear ideas that are easy to understand. When the manager role for the 24-7 Liaison Engineering team became vacant, I interviewed for the role. I can tell you in all honesty that I never wanted that job. But when I was interviewing for the role, I rattled off these three things as my vision for what I wanted to do with the group, should I be selected for the role.

In a way I had been hoodwinked into taking the job. Apparently, nobody else in the company had had a clear vision for that group, or else I was the only fool that had been suckered into interviewing for the job. I was in the Liaison Management role for three years and was able to work with the team to realize the visions I had. It was a slog of a three-year period, but it was nonetheless rewarding going in with a clear idea of what needed to be done and then seeing that idea worked through so that it became reality.

Many times, the person who has the best vision for a team is someone who, in all honesty, is the last person who actually wants to take on the job—especially if it is a tough job that needs to be done. Strong leadership candidates who work in other areas, particularly those who work downstream, can bring in a fresh outlook when internal candidates have become stale.

In the previous example, none of the managers in the 24-7 Liaison Engineering group thought they could justify getting the increase in headcount that would be required to develop the knowledge base that was needed to achieve the vision I had. But I had just come from a group where I had successfully built a lot of business cases justifying getting new resources because our fleet was growing, and the company understood that, with more airplanes, you need more people to keep them running. Ultimately, the company valued being able to fly more airplanes on time than it valued the incremental cost of adding a few extra engineers, especially if I could go out and get engineers fresh out of college and grow them internally into subject matter experts.

As I mentioned in the Preface, I've been accused of being lucky many times in my career. And I'll freely admit I have been quite lucky. But as I also alluded to, it's not *all* luck. I've learned a lot from the leadership at Delta. And one thing I learned over the years is the easiest way to convince a business that it needs to invest in resources is if you can start with a good vision, calculate how much it will cost to achieve that vision, and compare that to the benefit that the company will enjoy if your vision becomes reality. For instance, I watched our company make record profits year after year over the past decade after we decided to be a data-driven company. But that being said, you first have to have the vision to know what data to look at in order to sell a plan.

A lot of companies do a fairly pedestrian job of communicating a vision across a large employee base. Sometimes people try to do this by issuing mission statements or quality policies. Most employees couldn't tell you where to find a current copy of their mission statement. Heck, some can't even remember that their quality policy is hanging around their neck on the back of their badge. Even if they are aware of them, they are usually written in a way that requires an interpreter to translate them into plain language.

But at Delta, the vision for our company wasn't buried in corporate brochures and mission statements. Yes, we had both of those things, but any one of us could tell you what our brand was built on: it was all about the Delta people. We called it the "Delta Difference". Our leaders saw that we couldn't make enough of a profit by just offering a commodity. We flew the same airplanes as other companies to the same destinations using the same fuel, and we had to abide by the same strict regulations as all of the other majors. Our leaders recognized the fact that, to make profits, our customers needed to continue to choose to fly with us and to pay a premium to do so, even though they had several other choices.

It was drilled into us at every opportunity that we were better than the other airlines out there, not because we had better processes (we didn't always) or better airplanes (we flew really old airplanes compared to our competitors), but because we were Delta. We were special simply because all of us were the best people in the industry. Our secret sauce…was us!

Imagine how it made us feel to be told all the time by our leaders that we were the best people in the airline business. In a way, it was a self-fulfilling prophecy. If your employees constantly hear that they are the best, then they feel like they *are* the best. And when you *feel* that way, you begin to *act* that way.

Our company vision was so simple: in an industry that is highly commoditized, the vision was to differentiate our brand by focusing on the customer experience. If you have the best people in the industry focusing on bringing the customer the Delta Difference, then you've just ensured that most customers will have a great experience. As a leader, you've struck gold.

Once we all realized that our core mission was to delight the customer, it became very easy for all of us to start thinking in similar ways across the entire enterprise. The other key vision that went along with creating the Delta Difference was the idea that we needed to simplify the rules to make it easy for frontline employees and frontline leaders to make the right choices to please the customer.

For instance, Richard Anderson (Delta's CEO from 2007 to 2016) was well known for taking company manuals that had hundreds of pages of nonsense and getting them trimmed down to a dozen pages or less so that people could easily read and understand them. He argued that if people knew the intent of what you wanted them to do, you wouldn't need to micromanage every little decision they needed to make to have them fulfill those intentions. Anderson believed in simplicity and speed to market—that was his brilliance. He often reminded us that "speed wins," and that speed is the result of simplifying things.

Sometimes simplicity and speed just mean that you let the frontline agent listen to an angry customer who has just had their flight cancelled or their baggage lost while on their way to visit Aunt Mabel, who is on life support in Boston. Then, instead of making that agent go five layers of management up the chain in order to do the right thing, you let that frontline employee know management will have their back if they need to be "flexible" with the rules to do the right thing. And if it is clear and easy to understand that the rules already allow for that kind of flexibility, that's even better.

If the customer is in Atlanta with their luggage stuck somewhere in JFK, that agent should know that sometimes the right thing to do is to call up a trusted colleague in JFK to find the luggage and personally drive it up to BOS to meet the passenger so she can get some extra time with Aunt Mabel before she is taken off life support.

Obviously, you can't write this scenario down in an operation manual, and it wouldn't make sense to do this sort of thing except in exceptional circumstances. But if employees know that not only would they not get into trouble for doing this but also that they have leadership's support for doing it, you're more likely to have a network of agents who are willing to take this kind of risk when appropriate. If employees already know they are the "best people in the industry," they will take pride in going to huge lengths to show that off.

I heard so many accounts of employees doing things like this while I worked at Delta that I became a believer in the positive power that leaders wield, simply by making it easy to do the right thing. It's so important that all companies should make employee autonomy a part of their overarching vision, especially when it comes to customer service. This type of strategy can make you look like an absolute genius when your people are constantly out there trying to outdo each other with acts of kindness simply because you put the idea in their minds that they are the difference between our company and its competitors. And as a result, they are.

It's truly self-fulfilling.

As I have mentioned, one of the greatest things that Richard Anderson did early in his tenure as CEO of Delta was to take Delta people back to their roots. The basic vision for Delta in the early 21st century was basically a reboot of the vision that its founder set in the early 20th century. The strongest company visions are those that can transcend time and are connected with the brand itself. You can see how Richard Anderson's vision was actually an extension of C.E. Woolman's words: "The airline industry is keenly competitive. All of us have good planes, the only way in which we can excel is in the quality of our service. And this is where the human factor enters."

One other major vision that Delta had that transcends time is the idea that the employees of the company are a tight-knit family. It's such an ingrained philosophy that we all refer to ourselves, collectively, as the "Delta family." The concept originated from the vision that C.E. Woolman had nearly a century ago: "No one person is an airline. An airline is a team. It must be friendly, courteous, cooperative, efficient, and bound as closely as a devoted family."

When I first started my career, I would hear about the Delta family from the mechanics I worked with. They used to describe how it had been in the good old days. Most of the old-timers would tell me that the *real* Delta family was dead. You could have fooled me. I feel as close as brothers with the guys[5] I worked with all the way back to when I first started at Delta. Even today, after being apart from the mother ship for a few years, I feel that strong bond. When I go over to visit the shop that I was first hired into years ago, I feel like Norm Peterson walking into *Cheers*. It's like I never left.

I can't tell you how many people I've hired into Delta who later pulled me aside to tell me how different Delta is. The first time that happened to me, I must have responded with a funny look because the contractor who had told me said, "No, you really don't understand, Todd. This place is unlike anywhere else. People here really care about each other. That's not normal." It's still really hard for me to fully understand this, because I've never really worked anywhere else. But at the same time, it's kind of sad that I've heard it so many times. I take it for granted that everyone I work with knows my name, the name of my wife, the names of my kids, their ages, my hobbies, and so on. It's hard for me to envision working in a company that doesn't foster that type of relationship amongst the employees.

This is the power of vision for a leader. A simple vision, that is easy to understand and effectively communicated to a team, of being a tightly bound family can literally be the thing that sets your company, or your division or small group, apart

5 Yes, this group of guys did include females, as well. But on the shop floor, all of us tend to be "brothers" and "guys." And if I changed any pronouns here, my good friend Cecile would probably beat the crap out of me, so, for the sake of my own personal health, I'm going to stay away from doing that, if you don't mind.

from your peers—and this will last far beyond your time in your position or even beyond your own retirement. Even if you do nothing else, take the time to have a vision and make sure that you repeat it to the team time after time until they can put it into their own words and use it to shape their goals.

If you are interested in becoming a leader and making the transition from being a frontline employee to being a supervisor, manager, or beyond, make sure, above all, that you have a foundational idea of what you would like to do with the team before you apply for a leadership position. Remember that a good vision will get your team thinking for themselves about how they can establish good goals to realize the overarching idea. A great vision may last well beyond your time in office.

If you are the existing leader of a team, ask yourself these questions to check if you really have established a clear vision: What are the aspirations my team is striving to achieve? If I were to ask my team this same question, would they give the same answer I just did? You may even want to ask a few of your direct reports just to make sure your vision is coming across.

If you are trying to hire a leader, the easiest way to tell which candidates are worth considering is just by asking them what their vision is for your team. If they don't have one or you don't like what you hear, then don't hire them. But if someone comes along and has one that is well thought out and aligns with yours, then you may have something special.

It's that easy.

CHAPTER 2

Style Points Matter

Members of the Delta team have put the meaning in our slogan of Service and Hospitality from the Heart through teamwork.
–C.E. Woolman

I wear cowboy boots at work. I have several types: lizard skin, sharkskin, python, manta ray, ostrich, gator belly, and good old-fashioned cow leather. When I'm walking to and from my car in the morning and the evening, you'll see me in my brown, beaver-felt Stetson cowboy hat. In the cool weather months, I throw on a sport coat—my favorite is a light tan coat that clashes with everything except blue jeans. In my office, I like to keep a humidor full of cigars that I never smoke, next to an ashtray I never use. I wear a wide leather belt with a big, metal belt buckle with a big letter *T* on it. A lot of people call me "Tex"—even after I tell them I'm actually from California.

This wardrobe of mine is all a part of the style I've adopted in my work life. It's almost a character that I become when I go to the office. I invented this character almost a decade ago. It helps get me into the right mindset for who I need to be at work in order to get the people around me to respond to me in the way I need them to. When you're an engineer by trade, you need to be anything but a stereotypical engineer when you step into a management role—especially one where you need to go out to a hangar full of mechanics and machinists and work with a lot of folks who think we're all a bunch of nerdy, arrogant blowhards who can't relate to other human beings. And often they aren't wrong about that.

The character that I play at work is not entirely different from who I am outside of the office, but I will say that my persona at work is most certainly not the same persona I use with my wife and kids at home. To some extent, you have to adjust your persona and style to fit your audience, while still having it be a core part of who you are.

Granted, I look ridiculous in the hat, the boots, and the belt buckle. I know that, and most of you could have guessed that without even seeing the ensemble. But that's kind of the point. Nobody who sits down with me would ever confuse me for someone who thinks too seriously about himself. In fact, people are often disarmed and even chuckle a little when they look down and see I'm wearing snakeskins on my feet in the middle of a monthly performance meeting.

Richard Anderson used to wear high-water pants and blindingly colorful socks during his leadership meetings. There he'd be on stage sitting casually in a comfy leather chair in front of thousands of his frontline leaders, sharing his vision, and answering questions from his employees, and it was all you could do not to smile at his crazy socks. That was part of his style. He talked very frankly, very casually, wore a suit and tie, and had very loud socks.

Most leaders don't use bad wardrobe choices to accentuate their style in the workplace, but I need to tell you right now: style definitely matters! But I'm not talking about what you wear. I'm talking about the style you use to interact with your people (and your peers and leaders, too).

One of the things that frequent fliers remember about Richard Anderson was his warm southern drawl on the video that would play on every flight before the preflight safety video. He was reminiscing about Delta's rich history while sitting behind founder C.E. Woolman's desk. He wanted to personally welcome everyone aboard, and it almost felt like you were a personal guest on his airline. This went well with our heritage of being an airline built on hospitality and service from the heart.

Ed Bastian played a certain role and had a certain style when he and Richard Anderson were a team. Ed Bastian, the CFO of Delta (and a former banker), played the straight man in their two-man act. When both of them were on stage together, their opposing styles worked well together. They could take really tough questions from us and use their contrasting but complementary personas to say things that might not play well if delivered with what I'd call a typical "corporate" style. It was sometimes like watching Johnny Carson and Ed McMahon. You'd have to imagine Johnny Carson being sort of a bayou

Cajun, but you get the idea. They used that two-man routine very effectively to communicate with us.

That was something I learned by watching them—as leaders, you have an act you have to master. Sometimes you have to say some tough things to people, and your style will make a huge difference to how people perceive what you're telling them and, more importantly, how they'll react to what they are being told. As a leader, your style will make all the difference.

Of course, no one should try to be something different from who they actually are. But each of us does need to find a style that is already a part of us and accentuate those aspects of our personality that will help us relate best to our team. You ultimately have to figure out how to play your part, and the role you play needs to be practiced and well rehearsed.

For years, I had a boss who would come into our mezzanine every day, walk by each of our cubicles, and dish out creative insults. Most of the time, they were heavily laced with profanity. He did it to us all so consistently that if he came in and failed to insult you, you knew he was serious and would react appropriately. Funnily enough, this style worked for him[6].

One of my favorite parts of the day was when he'd come bebopping down the hall throwing his usual greetings out to everybody, and I'd have my own creative retort ready to throw back at him. I actually appreciated having a leader who treated us like he would treat his drinking buddies at the bar. It made

6 Even more amazing is the fact that he has a squeaky-clean Human Resources record. Maybe that goes to show you if you're consistent with your style, that's more important than what you say to people.

coming to work more fun, and I ended up working harder for that guy than I ever worked for anyone else.

It almost doesn't matter what a leader's style is, but as a leader, you've got to have one, it has to be yours, and you have to be consistent with it.

The more I watch old videos of C.E. Woolman, the more I am convinced that he totally understood the importance of adopting a personality style to help him lead his company. If you go back and watch a few old videos of him, you'll be convinced he grew up in the Louisiana low country. He didn't. He did move to Monroe, Louisiana, shortly after he graduated from college, but he spent the first 21 years of his life in Illinois!

As someone who is a transplant himself (I grew up in California and moved to Georgia to go to college), I can tell you that it is an active choice to adopt a southern accent. Your natural way of speaking, when you are alone, is usually how you spoke the first couple of decades of your life. My natural voice is kind of a mix between a California surfer and a Midwestern farmer. (My parents were both military brats, but they had deep familial roots in the Midwest). When I moved to the South, I certainly developed a bit of a southern twang, but I could turn it on and off, much like anyone else that moves here.

But it's interesting to listen to C.E. Woolman speak. Knowing that he was from Urbana, Illinois, and knowing he had lived there since shortly after his birth, I used to wonder why in all of his videos he chose to speak using a heavy southern

Louisiana accent. The simple answer is that he knew (as any transplant can tell you) that he could connect more with his people if he sounded more like them. Not everyone can pull that off well. I can kind of do it, but I'm also a little bit of a sponge for that sort of thing, as my wife will tell you. But the fact that a leader like C.E. Woolman spoke in an adopted southern accent and recognized that it gave him an ability to connect more with his people emphasizes how valuable it is for all leaders to adopt a style and use it to lead people. The style he adopted was critical because of his particular vision of providing "service and hospitality from the heart." How do you deliver that southern hospitality message to southern folk if you sound like a Midwesterner from Illinois?[7]

Now here's where I've got to be brutally honest. There are a lot of people in this world who just do not have any style at all. Many of them, for reasons related to ambition alone, think they need to become leaders to be successful in their careers. So, they take leadership roles. Then they take a corporate memo and read all of the "leader talking points" aloud to their teams but fail to put the message into their own words or to use their own style to deliver it. Essentially, all they are is a glorified corporate robot. This inspires exactly nobody.

People can tell when you lack style. When you just repeat what you heard someone else say or read from a script, that's not what being a leader actually means. There are some folks

---

7 It probably helped that his parents were natives of South Carolina. Our style has to come from part of who we really are. I'm guessing that Mr. Woolman felt a deep connection with the Southeast from an early age, but this is purely conjecture.

out there who honestly don't have the ability to bring their own flair to a role. If you suspect this might describe you, ask yourself why you want to become a leader. If it's truly because you have a vision for your department or company, then dig deep. Not everyone needs to be flamboyant, but every leader needs a style that is honest and that will appeal to your team and help you reach your vision.

Your style will help the people within your organization relate to you. If your people can't relate to you, then they won't trust you. This is why celebrities are hired to do commercials on TV. If you like a celebrity's style, you begin to relate to that person, so when that person tells you to buy a product they say is good, you trust them. But watch how fast the sponsor drops that celebrity when they go *out* of style.

Your team—no matter who they are—will want someone leading them who is more than just a person in a polo shirt and khaki pants. Everyone wants to have a leader with some personality. Your personality and style must be as reliable as a clock. People should never have to guess which version of you they'll be getting today. In some cases, it doesn't matter that much what that personality is, so long as it's consistent and it aligns with your vision.

If you work for a nonprofit organization and your vision is to bring charity and hope to impoverished people in war-torn nations, you may want to make sure that the style you bring to a leadership role there doesn't leave people mistaking you for Gordon Gekko. The "greed is good" style of leadership may work just fine if you are leading a team of traders on Wall

Street, but it wouldn't match that charity role that you took on, so do make sure that these two things align.

I can't overstate this point: whatever your style is, it has to be an extension of who you really are. It can't be a difficult act if you are going to put it on every day. If you try to pick a style that isn't natural, you're going to be spotted as a fake pretty easily. Don't be that person. Instead, just embrace whatever it is about your personality that makes you interesting to people. You might be interesting because you're a nerd. In that case, that can be a part of your personality. Own it. Go out and buy a pocket protector, put a couple of Star Trek figurines on your bookshelf, and be the best nerd you know how to be. Maybe you are a Marine and like to call people "sir" or "ma'am" and salute people in the hallways. That's fine too. Make sure that crew-cut stays high and tight and play the part right.

And if you are hiring someone for a leadership position, you've got to consider what style the candidate is going to bring to the group. A lack of style (or the wrong style) will erode trust more quickly than any other thing that a leader can lack. And if you don't have trust, you can't lead. Nobody will be following.

The chances are pretty high that if you can't recognize any style in a job candidate or you don't like the style you see during an interview (or while observing the candidate in their current role), the team members of the group that they will inherit won't either. I hate to say it, but human nature requires that people like you first in order for them to then want to help you succeed. Just ask yourself this: can you think of a boss you've had who you didn't like but you still wanted them to succeed? I can't think of a single one, and I've had 18 different bosses, so I should know. If you don't like someone's *style*, you're not going to like *them*.

Companies need to have a style too, one that stems from its vision. Delta has styled its brand throughout its history as a southern airline that brings its passengers real southern hospitality. Southwest Airlines styled itself with hot pants and knee-high boots in the 1970s. They've ditched the outfits, but they still maintain a style that grows out of their vision, which is to make the flying experience as fun as possible for their passengers. Virgin Atlantic became successful because it styled itself after its founder, Richard Branson. I think you're supposed to feel like you are a rock star if you fly with them.

Alaska Airlines maintains a cult following because their style involves being the "hometown airline" in the Pacific Northwest. It's not uncommon for a flight attendant to notice a crying baby being held by an exhausted mother and ask if they can hold it for a while. When you see a flight attendant bouncing up and down the aisle of a Boeing 737 holding a little baby (who is not crying any more), that lends to their hometown style and appeal. It's no wonder they enjoy fantastic customer loyalty. For years, we coveted Alaska's annual stranglehold on J.D. Power's award for customer satisfaction. Their style, when it comes to interacting with their passengers, is exactly why they win year in and year out.

All four of the carriers mentioned above actually have very similar company visions. Each of them knows that in order to win over loyalty from a consumer base that is essentially purchasing a commodity, your brand has to be different from the other brands that offer the same service. But they've all been highly successful at realizing their vision through four very different styles. And each of them adopted a style that fit part of who they really are. They didn't change their personalities. They took the best parts of their core and they accentuated those characteristics then encouraged their employees to embody those same characteristics to their passengers. The results speak for themselves.

On the other hand, without me sharing my opinion of them, how would you describe United Airlines' style? Do they have one? Do you think it's good? If you think it's good, do you watch the news or read social media?

Style certainly does matter to your brand. I'll leave it at that.

What your peers think about you can tell you a lot about how well your style is working. About five years ago, American Airlines (and later United Airlines) came out with a slogan to motivate their employees to beat Delta at whatever it was that was making us more profitable, punctual, customer focused, and so on. The slogan was KDA (short for "Kick Delta's Ass"). This really happened. They had bumper stickers and everything. At their leadership conferences, this acronym was actually cut into their leadership presentations to their managers. When that circulated back to *us*, we actually found it kind of flattering. The way we did business made such a difference that our fiercest competitors had teamed up to put a target on our backs. It was as if they jointly recognized we were in a class all by ourselves. We were setting a standard across the industry that was being acknowledged by the major carriers. Our response was to redefine what KDA really stood for: "*Kiss* Delta's Ass." (We meant it affectionately, of course).

There are times when your style won't fit with your team or your leader's style. If you can do something about that, do so. If not, it might be time to move on. I had the pleasure of working for a good friend of mine who was a unique and brilliant leader. Mike Kotas, who grew up in Buffalo, New York, led Delta's Cabin Maintenance team when I first started working closely with him. Mike grew up playing hockey, had suffered as a Bills fan for many years, and must have worn out his parents with his boundless energy. Some people at Delta called him "Hurricane Mike". He brought this whirlwind of northeastern energy everywhere he went, which either drove you crazy or inspired you to get things done. I found that if he drove you crazy, it meant you typically enjoyed a more laid-back environment and, as a result, your style was going to conflict with his. If you loved him, you typically loved rapid change and high velocity. Mike was the living personification of Richard Anderson's "speed wins" mantra.

What made his style work well, especially when he was leading the Cabin team, was the fact that he knew how to drive engagement for the frontline worker. He championed solutions to their problems, and his style was to call anyone out (even publicly) if they weren't working to fix those problems. He liked debate and enjoyed hearing differing opinions, so his morning meetings typically had a large audience and his divisional monthly performance reviews were even larger. He also wasn't shy about admitting when he had been wrong (and even doing this publicly).

Although he tended to be critical if you came to him with the same problems day to day or month to month, he was consistent in his methods, which made his style fair. He kept you on your toes, and you could expect to get an earful if you didn't take action on commitments you had made. But he kept the same style, no matter what, so everything was predictable, from the lively meetings to the straight talk.

Mike was really good at working his team into a frenzy. I remember that at a couple of Christmas parties that he threw for his team in downtown Atlanta, it was almost like watching Leonardo DiCaprio's depiction of Jordan Belfort in the war room in *The Wolf of Wall Street* (minus the Quaaludes and money laundering, of course). You could tell that some of his guys would gladly run through a brick wall for him. It's no wonder why Delta's cabins became the cleanest and best maintained passenger environments our industry had ever experienced.

Mike gave his team a reason to come in and care about their job. You knew that if you did something well, he was going to notice it and he was going to tell people about it. If you kept doing it well, you knew you were going to be given more responsibility and maybe even earn the opportunity to lead one of his teams. You also knew that if you didn't put in your best efforts, he was going to notice it, and it would be discussed. If you kept that trend going in the wrong direction, you'd have responsibilities removed and might not be leading one of his teams for very long. So, people tended to pay attention to what they were doing.

Mike knew not everyone liked his style, but he also correctly estimated that a lot of people did. He calculated that it worked more times than it didn't, and he created a world-class organization out of what had previously been a rag-tag group with no identity. Most of his employees loved him, and more than a few tears were shed at the local watering hole when he left the group to join Delta's Aircraft Maintenance Planning team.

A couple of years later, I went to work for him. This was right before he got another promotion to Airport Customer Service (ACS) across the street. I only got to work with him as his direct report for three months, but it was possibly my favorite three months at Delta Air Lines. His style was infectious, and it made me feel bolder than I had previously been. When he left to go over to ACS, I found out the hard way that, when your leader leaves and you get a new leader, your style sometimes needs to adjust as well. With Mike at the helm, I could play off of his energy and match his confidence level. When I got a new boss, that level of intensity and boldness just didn't work. I struggled for the next three months and actually decided to leave that role because I wasn't the right fit, stylistically, with my new boss.

As with anything, you have to know when it's time to do something different in your career. The higher you go in management, the more you need to ask yourself whether or not your ways of doing business are compatible with the leaders above you. If they're not, you need to find something else.

Realistically, your ability to change your style is going to be very limited. Everyone has some room for maneuvering, but it's not infinite. The same is true of the leader you report to and the leaders underneath you—ultimately, you are who you are. If anyone in Human Resources tries to tell you differently, they are grossly mistaken and are giving you false hope of being able to stay in a position for which your personality style isn't appropriate.

It's really critical to pay attention to everyone's style and how they work together when you are creating a team of leaders. The worst thing you can do for your company is to put a bunch of leaders together that have styles that clash. They may all be great in their own ways in different environments, but if their styles will make it hard for them to work together, do yourself a favor and say no to bringing them all on board. Similarly, if someone above you wants to force someone with a clashing style onto your team because they "need a home," you'd better push back hard before it ruins the dynamic of the team you've worked so hard to build. Ultimately, the people you value most will be the ones who recognize that the team isn't working any more. They're the ones who usually bail out on you first—and they are rarely the people you actually want to lose.

Developing the right style for your company, your division, your team, and for yourself as a leader, is critical to driving the overall vision. A vision, sitting on a piece of paper, needs your flair to bring it alive so that everyone engaged in the mission can connect with it. The right style will attract good people who believe in what you are doing. Yes, they liked the vision, but they only felt that vision come alive when you were able to show them that it is more than words on a piece of paper—that it is part of the core of who you are, as a leader; it's ingrained in your division and your team, and it is the driving force behind everything your company does.

CHAPTER 3

Setting Goals (Not Deadlines)

We are buying airplanes that haven't yet been fully designed with millions of dollars we don't have and are going to operate them off airports that are too small, in an air traffic control system that is too slow, and we must fill them with more passengers than we have ever carried before.
–C.E. Woolman

I had a good friend who decided he wanted to retire early. He set a goal for himself to become a millionaire by the age of 35 to help him achieve this vision. His plan was to save as much money as he could while still enjoying a reasonable lifestyle and raising a family. He sought a couple of promotions at work to help him put even more into savings along the way, and he never spent a dime of his annual bonus checks. His investment plan was fairly high-risk, but he figured that it was worth taking some risks while he was young enough to recover from any failures he might have. He drove really inexpensive cars (and always bought them used), he didn't buy expensive clothes, he avoided expensive habits, and he did all of his own work on his house, which was very modest.

A few of my friend's investments didn't pan out exactly as he had hoped, and, ultimately, he didn't hit his goal of having his net worth reach a million dollars by the age of 35. He didn't lose focus, though, and remained diligent, and he did eventually get there. However, he had to wait until he was 39—just a few months away from his 40th birthday—to get to where he wanted to be. Now, here's the question: did he fail to reach his goal?

Well, some of you out there will recognize that he did, technically, fail to reach his goal. Some might say he failed miserably. After all, he missed his goal by a whopping four years! When he set his goal, he was already 30 years old, so he overran his target by almost 100%. What a loser, right? The rest of you might respond: "Are you nuts? The guy's a millionaire!" Well, the truth of it lies somewhere in between. But one thing is for sure: if my friend had never set a goal for himself, he probably would have been prone to do what most people do, which is to spend nearly every dime he had instead of saving to become a millionaire.

In the end, it's pretty tough to say whether my friend feels good about himself or not. If I knew more about his vision, that could help me guess whether he was satisfied with his timeline or not. For example, if his vision was to be able to quit his job and feel financially secure enough to teach high school for the rest of his career and never worry about saving for retirement on a teacher's salary, then I'd feel fairly confident that his overrun wasn't that significant. If he wanted to do all of that and then totally stop working by the time he was 45 so he could start racing Ferraris, then he might be feeling differently right now. That's part of why vision matters: you can only tell if you've been successful in hitting your goals if you understand the overarching mission.

Most of us would probably recognize that my friend benefitted from the fact that he had sat down and set a goal for himself. And, again, if he hadn't spent the time setting that goal, it'd only have been blind luck if he ever reached it. The vast majority of people out there would look at my friend and say, "Congrats, and a job well done, Sir." That's what I'd personally say to him, anyhow.

When setting a goal, it's important to first make sure that, if you hit it, you are further along the path to achieving what you set out to achieve when you sat down and outlined your vision. Visions and goals go hand in hand. A lot of people confuse vision with goals because the two are so closely connected. Let's be very clear, though—they are distinctly different. As mentioned previously, a vision is high level and directional. It is not really measurable along the way. A goal is something you need to at least be able to measure somewhere along the journey toward realizing a vision.

If I were stranded on a deserted island, I'd have a vision of eventually sitting comfortably in my home. Can I measure my progress toward realizing that vision? Not really. Without some goal to help me measure progress, I'm just stranded on the deserted island, at home sitting comfortably on my couch, or somewhere in between. But unless I'm home safely already, I can't really tell you if I was doing well or if I was even moving in the right direction toward my vision.

If one of my goals to achieve that vision had been to build a boat before hurricane season so I could sail to safety, could I measure that? Sure. I could tell you that I was 50% done with the construction of my boat and that hurricane season was due to start in three months. If I had started building my craft a month-and-a-half earlier, I could, at least, estimate my chances of meeting my goal. Without knowledge of other factors, like the availability of material, the complexity of the tasks still to be done, or the skills required to complete the task (for instance whether I have them or not), all of which I've given no information about, you'd be able to draw a reasonable conclusion that I am probably on target for success.

Now, if a storm ripped through the island a day before I was scheduled to complete my boat, and I lost everything and had to start over, my goal could be beyond reach. Can I still achieve my vision? Of course, I can. Do my goals need to change? Almost certainly. My goal might for instance transition into setting the island on fire before the next cruise ship sailed by in the hope that someone would see it and come to rescue me. But if I do nothing and set no goals, the chances of me getting off that island are pretty slim.

In the same way, we have to think of goals in the workplace as tools to help us achieve our vision. Many times, we don't really know if our goals are achievable. That's okay. A goal is not a plan. You may set several goals this year that are so outlandish nobody in the world could achieve them. But if you don't know for sure that it isn't possible, then it may still be a reasonable goal for the team until you figure that out. It is a calculated risk at that point. So long as the reward would be exponentially more valuable than the resources you spend pursuing a really stretched target, then sometimes that's fine.

When I was serving on a temporary assignment in Delta's Fleet Projects group, I was given several goals that seemed borderline impossible to me. Our project group was the one that took all of the crazy ideas that corporate came up with and figured out the feasibility, timeline, and cost of implementing them across Delta's fleet. Examples of these projects include retrofitting cabins to make old interiors look new and fresh and installing modern features, like full-spectrum LED lighting, 2Ku Wi-Fi antennas, slim-line seats, audio/video on-demand (AVOD), and other amenities that come as standard on new modern aircraft.

In 2016, a request came down from our COO, Gil West, that at first glance I thought was entirely absurd. On second glance, I thought it was merely preposterous. But after sitting down with some experts and re-evaluating it with the team, we all agreed: it was the most insane idea we had ever heard, and we'd all be out of our minds to sign up to do it.

Gil West was known at Delta for being somewhat of a riverboat gambler. But he was actually really good at figuring out which ideas were worth the risk of pursuing. He told my future boss, Rick Salanitri (who, at the time in the summer of 2016, was my in-house supplier), that he wanted us to develop a new In-Flight Entertainment (IFE) system from scratch and have it ready for installation onto Delta's newly purchased Bombardier C-Series fleet. This fleet was originally set to start delivery to Delta in early 2018.

To put this into perspective, it usually takes an established IFE company around three years to develop a new system and get it certified for commercial aircraft installation. We were not an established IFE company. If fact, we had exactly zero employees who had any background in designing or manufacturing such a system. Oh, and did I mention that this was also supposed to be the world's first *wireless* system? Yeah, so all the content would also be wirelessly transmitted from the Cabin Management System to each tablet mounted in the seatbacks. Nobody had ever tried this before. In fact, nobody even knew if this was possible! Rick originally said no to this mad plan.

Something that people who work for Gil West eventually learn about him is that he likes to play a little game[8]. The game consists of this: If he doesn't get the answer he wants from you, he will sometimes ask you to take off your company badge and put it on the table in front of you. He'll then instruct you to only pick your badge back up (which would imply that you don't want to be fired) if you agree to pursue the goal that

---

8 Admittedly, I only know this secondhand, but I've heard it from so many Delta leaders who have had to play this "game" with Gil West, that I'm sure it's true. Rick tells us this story so often that it's part of division folklore.

he had laid out for you—the one you already told him wasn't going to work. He did this to Rick in the summer of 2016. And Rick picked his badge back up, which meant that all of us were on the hook to somehow figure out a way to achieve this mad goal.

Rick had come to Delta from a company called the *HAECO Group* in Greensboro, North Carolina. He was hired into Delta to build a division that would focus on designing and manufacturing cabin interior retrofit kits, just like he had done at his old employer for 20-something years. In 2016, a wholly owned subsidiary company was registered in a filing cabinet in the great state of Delaware, called *Delta Flight Products, LLC* (DFP). Rick became the president of DFP and, before his separate little company even got off the ground, this big albatross called Wireless IFE was tied around his neck! And, by extension, mine too!

Rick pulled me aside sometime in October of that year and told me he didn't think we'd hit our target of delivering the IFE system in time for the first aircraft in early 2018, as Gil had wanted. More than likely, he told me, we'd be better to plan on hitting aircraft number eleven given all of the research, development, and testing that needed to be done. Well, since he was now the company expert on the matter, I figured I'd trust him. So, I rounded up everyone in the Junior Fleet Subcommittee from all around Delta, and I pitched four different options, making the fourth option the one where we burn all of our boats and go all-in on this untested and unproven wireless IFE solution that we weren't even sure physics would support.

The first option I sketched up was to install blanking plates on the first ten airplanes and then start installing our system by the time we were ready. Passengers would be staring at a piece of plastic instead of a TV screen on the first ten airplanes, but they wouldn't know any difference. IFE didn't even come standard on the C-Series airplane, so there was no big loss there. Later on, we'd replace the piece of plastic with the tablets that we would be designing, and all would be groovy. This was the option I liked best—it was super low risk and gave us time to get a good cut-in for success.

The second option was to approach Panasonic, the IFE provider on the rest of Delta's fleet at that time and tell them we wanted them to install their standard IFE package on the first 35 aircraft, and then we'd take on the next 35-plus airplanes using our system. At least the passengers would have in-flight entertainment, even though it was a substantially more expensive option. For the passenger experience, I thought this was the best option, as it guaranteed they'd have entertainment on Day One. It would be highly expensive, though, as the Panasonic system was not cheap.

The third option involved developing a completely wired system, which would at least limit our risks a bit by eliminating the variable of the wireless system's physical construction infeasibility. But this option would add a couple hundred pounds of weight, which would increase fuel costs. The wires also were likely to go bad over time necessitating field replacement, which adds more maintenance costs, and they would be more expensive overall. The Panasonic system also had coaxial wire harnesses, so this was no worse than that option, but it was still riskier than going with their system because we hadn't developed the dang system yet.

And the fourth option—the one we all hated—was to go for broke and develop the full-on wireless variant... and make damn sure to have it ready for aircraft number one. Gil West chose option number four, which we had been insisting was the worst option available. He was hell-bent on burning all his ships! I watched, nervously, as the Niña, Pinta, and Santa María lay burning in the harbor. We were stuck in Gil West's New World without a ship in which we could sail home.

Seeing as our fates were intertwined, I figured I'd be better off going and joining this rabble band of DFP entrepreneurs, which would at least give me more control of my fate. So, on January 1, 2017, I became employee number one[9] of this new subsidiary, taking the role of Director of Quality and Safety at DFP.

My department, on Day One, consisted of me, myself, and I. I had gone from managing an $800 million+ annual budget for capital aircraft programs with a staff of three managers and over 30 project managers to being a lone ranger with a mission to build a team that would oversee one of the most well-funded startup companies in the history of aviation.

For the first year, knowing our mission which involved the vision of creating the world's first wireless IFE system while

9 A somewhat pedantic technicality seems required here: Rick and all of his direct reports remained Delta Air Lines, Inc. employees. I was hired on the same day as five other DFP employees. But since I had the highest seniority within Delta among the six of us that shared a January 1 start date, I was listed on the Human Resources roster as employee number one. That is a factoid I'll be sure to tell my grandchildren!

simultaneously delivering on our first FAA-approved cabin retrofit program on Delta's Boeing 777-200, the DFP leaders work-shopped our company goals together. We came up with several goals—and most of them seemed impossible. The first was to deliver our IFE system to Bombardier for entry into service on the first C-Series aircraft[10] before the end of 2017. The second was to deliver the first major prototype modification kit (which involved 72 sub-kits, and thousands of parts) for the aforementioned 777-200 modification (and have it inspected and approved for installation by the FAA). And the third was to create a quality management system by midyear for a facility that we would not move into until May of the same year. Oh, and we had to design the new building too. Did I mention we also wanted to implement a new Enterprise Resource Planning (ERP) system?

Looking back at what we wrote down for our goals in the early parts of 2017, I'd say we were legitimately crazy. Nobody on the planet would have thought that even half of these goals would have been logical for a new startup company, let alone the entire gamut. The only thing that I can say is that at least we all went into 2017 knowing what we were signing up for. None of us could have looked back after failing to do all the things we agreed to do and said we hadn't had our eyes wide open heading into the storm. We were all big boys and girls, and we had all signed on the dotted line knowing what we were committing ourselves to do. I guess we were all a little off kilter.

---

10 The C-Series design would be later sold to Airbus and rebranded the Airbus A-220. Officially, the Type Certificate from the FAA was issued against the BD-500.

The entire 2017 calendar year was a blur. It was fast paced. It was exhilarating. And it was absolutely nuts. There is a reason nobody had tried all of this before. And the simple reason is that it actually required a certain amount of stupidity and raw stubbornness even to attempt what we bit off. It also required a customer foolish enough to finance all of it and be patient enough to watch as we flirted with failure for the better part of the year. Delta Air Lines was just that sort of customer.

Yes, we did move into our building on time: goal number three ticked off the list. That's the one thing that went swimmingly well. We did get a quality management system in place before the end of July, as well. However, to be honest, that was more about sitting down and writing rules rather than exercising them. Getting people to follow our new rules would take the better part of the next two years to master.

Late summer and fall of 2017 was a busy time as we had just implemented a software rollout of SAP's Enterprise Resource Planning (ERP) software, which all of us hated. (SAP is short for Systems Applications and Products in Data Processing and also the name of the company who marketed this particular ERP.) SAP is fine, if you configure it well, but we hadn't spent the time or money necessary to do a full implementation. Halfway into our implementation, we decided to cut bait and go with the ERP system that all of us had wanted from the beginning, which was called Epicor. This was the system everyone had used in previous companies before joining DFP, and it was built for the smaller, more nimble kind of company that we were. Mother Delta used SAP, so it had kind of been shoved down our throats from

Day One. We eventually convinced the powers-that-be that we'd be able to dovetail our new Epicor system into SAP so they could do their month-end financial close on time, but it was a battle getting them to accept it.

With a half-assed SAP implementation in hand, we went full throttle to implementing Epicor. And we only had three months to do it before we needed to start delivering product for the 777-200 modification program. Most companies recommend allowing a full 12 months to implement a new ERP system. I understand why, now. We sat down and ground through it all and came out with a system that was at least functional by November.

Looking back, rushing through this implementation was probably our biggest mistake. We should have given ourselves a lot more time to implement our ERP system. It is just so critical that you do that. Your ERP system is the fundamental financial and operational building block to any manufacturing company, and everyone in the company needs to really know how it works in order for it to be a useful and trustworthy tool. We just didn't have the time, so it simply wasn't an option to delay. We released a functional version of our ERP system and we continued to modify it as we went—sort of like building an airplane while you're flying it. And then we moved on to the next step: becoming an approved Airbus supplier.

Wait, what? When did Airbus enter the picture? That wasn't one of our goals! Why now? Oh, right—because we worked for Gil West. Yeah, so Gil thought we didn't have enough to worry about in our inaugural year at DFP. So, he signed us up to certify a new IFE system on a new fleet Delta had ordered from Airbus—the beautiful new A330-900 Neo. I'm not even going to begin describing the complexity that this new program brought to our little business, but needless to say, now Airbus was about to get into our hair. And fast!

To make a long story short, the IFE program we were working on for the C-Series jets was largely a joint effort between DFP, who were responsible for supplying the touch screen monitors; Gogo, who provided the software and cabin management unit that delivered the content to and controlled the Graphical User Interface (GUI) on the monitors; and a hardware/wire-harness provider called Astronics. Each of us had our distinct roles, and we were focused on our individual pieces of that program. On the new A330-900 Neo program, DFP was to own the whole system, including designing the GUI and the in-seat wire harnesses. There was one major obstacle: we didn't have software engineers, and we'd never designed a GUI.

These Airbus guys do not mess around, and they are not inclined to allow a manufacturer of cabin equipment to get in the way of moving their airframe assembly line every day. The penalty for shutting down their production is substantial! They made this super clear to us when their Top Scan review team showed up in September for a program review. Not that we had any program plan to review with them at that time, which they noted in their outgoing report. That was fun to explain to management.

Fortunately, right about this time we picked up a great leader from Rockwell Collins named Alice Belcher. Alice was an IFE guru who started to put a team together that had tons of Airbus IFE experience, and she got us on a path to success real quickly. Alice built a team and brought in much-needed structure to our IFE design team. The first piece of evidence I saw that Alice was a great leader was how she was able to pull many of the talented people she knew she needed from Southern California and get them to move to Atlanta. When they got their calls from her, they didn't hesitate to come out. And it was because of her. They knew she would bring success. Above all, though, she brought calmness to the program that translated into confidence in the team that they could engineer a pathway to success. She was a great shot in the arm for the team.

(Incidentally, I don't mind if I take a small amount of credit for her coming aboard by begging Rick to hire her after she came out to Atlanta to interview for her VP role. She taught me a lot about leading people during the three years I worked with her. I had the pleasure of working directly for her for about two months before I retired, and she helped me make the toughest decision of my career, which was to move on.)

Despite the reinforcements starting to trickle in, our heads were spinning a bit at that time. We still had to focus on delivering our 777-200 program that was due to ship out right before Christmas (Friday, December 15, to be exact). Remember the FAA-approved cabin retrofit program, goal number two? As shipments started to pile onto our docks in November, I started to calculate the number of inspections we had to do in that short time period. I began to kiss Christmas vacation goodbye as the timeline grew closer and closer. My team started in late November, giving up on weekends and evenings and just planning on being in the office doing First Article inspections on all of the thousands of parts that made up those 72 sub-kits.

We ended up missing our deadline. Totally my fault. I was the end-of-line guy, and I didn't finish up the final inspections on time. Friday, December 15 came and no shipment was made. We shipped Monday, December 18, instead. It was a mild setback, and the champagne would have to remain on ice over the long weekend, but my Christmas, at least, was saved. Our first major shipment was on its way to get packed onto a slow boat over to China. Actually, it was Singapore, but same difference, distance-wise. What a year! But shoot—we still needed to deliver the IFE System, goal number one!

Our brand-new, touch-screen tablets, which were really the big development piece for us on this IFE system, had been designed in partnership with *Hitachi High-Tech America, Inc.*, out of Greenville, South Carolina. When I heard we were working with Hitachi, I thought we were working with Mother Hitachi, the huge electronics techno-giant. What I didn't expect was to find was a rag-tag group of less than 20 employees working in a small mom-and-pop-like factory in the middle of nowhere, South Carolina.

To give proper credit, the folks up in the Greenville plant are extremely talented. Their leadership and I just had very different ideas about things like configuration control and quality assurance procedures. I had told them in July that I wouldn't be accepting any units to flow through to our customer (Bombardier) until we got a full materials and parts traceability report on our First Article units[11] . I also told them we needed a formal agreement that stated they would notify us of any changes to their product, even if one little resistor changed on their motherboard. Apparently, they thought this was optional. Sadly, it wasn't.

One of our biggest goals of the year was to deliver our first ship-set of tablets, Integrated Tablet Units (ITUs), before December 31. The only thing standing in our way, at the end of the day, was our First Article paperwork, which hadn't been started, and a Notice of Change Agreement that had been sitting on Hitachi's legal team's desk for several months. I stuck to my guns and refused acceptance until we got both of those things done. December 31 came and went, and they weren't done. Once again, we were close to hitting our goals, but not quite there, and in retrospect I realized I should have pushed them harder to complete the paperwork before it hit crisis stage.

Over the Christmas break, boy did I get some phone calls. Goals that are tied to calendar years (and financial goals, to boot) are a big deal when you don't hit them. Even bleeding into 2018 by a single day would have caused consternation. The team had worked so hard to hit this milestone, and we couldn't deliver because the paperwork wasn't done. In aviation, the records of the manufacturing are as important as the quality

---

11 First Articles are the first manufacturing lot off the manufacturing line. You have to produce a report for every individual part that details out the proof that you have successfully met every single requirement that is listed on the engineering blueprint. A First Article Inspection Report (FAIR) can be hundreds of pages of records that have to be catalogued, checked, and approved by the manufacturer of record, which, in this case, was DFP. For reference, the industry standard that defines FAIR requirements is AS9102.

of the actual parts. Without having complete records, your parts are worthless. I didn't have my records, so my customer didn't get their parts.

It ended up taking an extra 30 days to get the paperwork all tidied up to ship. There were many phone calls required with subcontractors and sub-subcontractors in Taiwan, Japan, Malaysia, and all across the United States just to get all of the configuration control data and records that we needed. And we did get it. Every last bit. We held to what our QMS had said we were supposed to do, and we verified every single resistor, capacitor, and touch-screen component in that ITU. And then we delivered our system, complete, to Bombardier.

At that point, a dose of reality hit: the entire C-Series program got delayed. Apparently, we weren't the only subcontractor that was having issues on that aircraft. I heard there were significant delays with the engines, some of the cabin interior's parts, and several other systems. And we hadn't even gotten to the seats yet. The seats that would have our ITUs installed in them still had to go through Head Impact Criteria (HIC) testing, which is FAA/CAA-required [12] before getting certified. This is where you run a sled down a track and have it simulate a crash, and crash test dummies are slammed into the seat in front of them right where the ITU is installed. That all still had to happen, so even *we* weren't out of the woods yet.

---

12 Civil Aviation Authorities (CAA) is a collective term for all foreign regulatory authorities that oversee aviation safety requirements. EASA, Transport Canada, and the UK CAA are all examples. In this case, the original CAA was Transport Canada since the C-Series aircraft had originally been certified by Bombardier.

But we had delivered. Yes, it was a full month late. Yes, some people were really upset that we hadn't hit our mark exactly on time. But holy mole—consider what we'd just done! We completed virtually every one of our ill-advised goals. And nearly on time! And on top of that, we'd hired about 120 employees over that one-year period, which, if you've ever done a lot of hiring, takes up a rather large chunk of your day. Our lone HR manager had had quite the challenge that year with on-boarding all of us.

If you just looked at a line in the sand, and you measured our success solely based on whether or not we hit a date ahead of that line, you'd say we failed to meet our deadlines. And you'd be absolutely right. You might think that means we were unsuccessful overall. But in this case, you'd be so very wrong. Setting draconian, unmovable deadlines forces you to compromise your product. That's not what we did. We delivered a good product. The product we delivered is flying today. And it is high quality and very safe. I still feel proud of that fact.

As leaders, we don't measure success against meaningless deadlines when we know virtually nothing about what it is going to take to reach our target date. We know the vision, set goals, and work diligently toward those goals, and that's what we did. Every month, the Executive team got together and reviewed our progress toward achieving our goals. We took feedback from those performance reviews and met divisionally and changed our plans, as necessary, based on the feedback from the Executive team. Then, every week, each manager measured progress toward each goal with their team (which we'll discuss in greater detail in subsequent chapters). With that simple strategy, we got a lot of complicated things done in a short amount of time. When it comes down to it, there's not a sane company in the world that would have tried to do what we attempted. And even if some out there would have tried, we're the only ones who can say we did it!

Looking back, this little team we put together was responsible for doing some monumentally bold things. We built a wireless IFE system, the first of its kind in the world. And it works: and, by George, it works well! We got our first FAA Parts Manufacturing Approval a year after we moved into our building and six months after we opened on-site production. We got certified under ISO9001 and AS9100, which is the gold standard for aerospace manufacturers in the fall of 2018. Later that same fall, Airbus approved us as a manufacturer for IFE systems for line-fit installation, and DFP has been supplying parts to them ever since without issue. We never slowed down their production line and were never given any penalties.

We were able to achieve some pretty impossible things because we set such challenging goals. Had Gil West not believed in us so much, we'd never have challenged ourselves as much as we did. His genius in riverboat gambling was really all about assessing his people and believing in us being able to do anything he felt was humanly possible. After all, we were the *best* people in the industry[13]! Had Rick not picked up his

---

13 I actually made this a part of our Quality Policy and printed it on the back of a laminated card that hung on the back of each of our badges: "DFP people are the *best* in the industry - committed to safety and quality every day. We expect excellence, though: supplying superior solutions, a determination to deliver, and through a culture of continuous improvement."

badge and taken the challenge from Gil West, we'd never have gone anywhere. To be fair to Rick and to myself, after HIC testing finally got resolved on the C-Series program, you know what aircraft we really would have hit if they hadn't delayed their airframe production? Number eleven. But in his calculus, I think Gil West really knew that the first airplane was never going to be ready in January of 2018. After all, since when are airplanes manufacturers ever on time?

The types of goals that we put together at the beginning of our journey were fairly high level. The measurements we took each month to track where we thought we were versus how far we had left to go were based on a task versus timeline plot. We knew what tasks needed to be completed, and we knew the dates we wanted to get everything done by, so we were simply just looking at keeping up each month with where we had forecasted we needed to be at that end. This wasn't an exact science, and it wasn't very sophisticated, either. But it goes to show you that, even without a ton of heavy thinking, even a simplistic set of goals can drive you to stay so focused on the end that it's almost hard not to meet your objectives. Human nature dictates that people gravitate toward figuring out how to get a solution when you give them a clear enough picture of what you are trying to do and when you want it.

Having clear goals gives your team the ability to laser-focus on an objective. Without a clear goal, you can have a team full of rock stars, and you'll go nowhere. Goals become powerful when they are measurable. This is particularly the case when you can set meaningful targets that are relevant to the ongoing health of your business. Unlike goals that are event based, like the examples we just saw of measuring your progress toward completion of a big project, health indicators are simply ongoing measurements that you can take at any snapshot in time. Structuring goals around things you continually measure that tell you how well your company or division is performing are commonly known as Key Performance Indices (KPIs). Delta has become a very data-driven, goal-based organization in the last decade. This allowed them to even more successfully drive positive trends by using KPIs. This was particularly true within the operations teams.

The Technical Operations (Tech Ops) team really started to put the pedal to the metal, ironically enough, after we had had one of the most abysmal summer performances in recent memory back in 2010. We had so many cancellations that year that we decided to create some goals that focused on making sure that would never happen again. Delta decided to start to measure what we called Maintenance Cancel-Free Days. These are calendar days across the entire enterprise where Tech Ops is not to blame for a single cancellation due to maintenance issues. We had zero of these days in 2010. In fact, Delta had to cancel over 5,600 flights in 2010 due to maintenance issues. That's a lot of cancellations and a whole lot of angry customers. Over 15 cancellations per day, on average!

In 2011, we started to zero in on a target at Tech Ops: no cancellations due to maintenance. We looked at all of the reasons that we had cancelled flights in the previous few years.

We had too few spare aircraft in the heavy flying months. We didn't have the right spare parts at the right stations. Our rescue parts provisioning system was broken. Our engineering teams weren't staffed correctly to handle non-routine request call volumes. The planning teams didn't have a clear strategy on what the daily plan was going to be. Systematically, we had just been tolerating the idea that flights routinely get cancelled due to unforeseen maintenance issues. We had not adopted a zero-defect expectation for our operation yet. We had not created a KPI to show us what our target should look like.

From 2011 onward, as an organization, we started to really pay attention to the numbers that drove cancellations. We figured out that a really good day started with every aircraft making its first flight out on time. As an engineer, I was invited to a management presentation of some of the metrics that we would start to focus on. Lee Gossett, who would become our VP of Line Maintenance, introduced a bunch of charts to the Tech Ops team showing some of the trends of KPIs that we needed to improve. One of the KPIs Lee wanted us to hone in on was First Flight *D*0, which is the rate at which your Departure time, *D*, left zero minutes behind schedule. The more we focused on making sure our *first* flight of the day went smoothly, the fewer downstream flights were impacted. One thing that's easy to see is that when you cancel that first flight or it gets heavily delayed, the chances of the rest of the flights that day leaving on time is significantly decreased. Some of the narrow-body fleets get up to eight flight cycles every day, so that's a huge downstream impact.

Lee also focused in on deferrals. A deferral is when you are legally allowed by the FAA to put off doing something like replacing a broken lavatory recirculation fan or a passenger seat reading light. Obviously that lavatory fan or reading light being broken isn't going to hurt anyone, but you're required to fix that broken part within a mandatory time period. Ultimately, you can't have everything on board broken all the time, or else the flight crew has to spend an inordinate amount of time managing broken things instead of focusing on their job, which is to keep passengers safe.

For that reason, the FAA does make you hold to those established time frames. So, the more airplanes you have out there that are flying with deferred maintenance tasks, the more tasks you have that need to get scheduled to be done within, say, a one-day, three-day, or ten-day period, depending on what you are deferring.

If you have half of your fleet flying around with open deferrals, you're rolling the dice that each airplane is going to be able to be scheduled in for some downtime during that mandatory period to fix it. It becomes hard to manage, and there are more chances for someone to drop the ball. Consequently, we started to focus on making sure we kept the total number of open deferrals low, even tracking how many were out there on their last day. Those became goal-based metrics for us to hit as a team. A new KPI was born.

By the same logic, if you get above a certain number of airplanes that are scheduled to be flying but are out of service, the chances are you will run out of operational spare airplanes to cover the flight schedule. We also kept statistics on how many aircraft we had at any given time that were out of service but were *unscheduled* out-of-service aircraft. We created a goal around that total number and started to drive that number down, month by month. To start with, we took our current metrics, knocked them down by a couple numbers, and figured out how to reach that goal. Then, when we figured out more efficiencies, we knocked it down again. Aircraft Out-of-Service (AOS) was a number we all kept on our monitors 24-7 in every operations support area. We started to keep tabs on what drove the AOS event, too. And someone at Delta had goals based on the number of times each type of thing that drove an AOS event occurred.

There were several more of these KPI-based metrics that we all started to train ourselves to watch. We knew when we had had a good day or a bad day, not by looking at how many delays or cancellations we had had. We watched the things that *led* to delays or cancellations. We became a lean, mean, metrics-based, goal-driven operational machine. And boy, did we start smoking the rest of the industry when we figured out how to drive those leading indicators down!

We started to see results as soon as 2011. We all marched to the same goal of zero cancellations. We could now put a number on it and watch as we closed in on each target. When we got to the KPI level we had established for 2011, we ratcheted up the goal and refocused our efforts. Rinse and repeat that process over a seven-year period and, by 2017, Tech Ops had managed one of the greatest maintenance feats in commercial aviation history.

That year, we had 324 days out of 365 with zero maintenance cancellations! Remember that in 2010, we hadn't even had one single day that was cancel free. In fact, we got so good at running such a reliable schedule that by mid-decade other major carriers started accusing us of cooking the books. So, we showed them the data, and that's about when they started their KDA (*Kick Delta's Ass*) campaign. In our industry, all of these stats are monitored closely by the US Department of Transportation, so you really can't hide your performance data. It's all there for the public to digest. You can argue about who has better block-time efficiency or whether looking at *A*0 (percentage of arrivals that land at or prior to schedule) versus *A*15 (percentage of flights that arrive at or prior to fifteen minutes later than scheduled) is more meaningful, but the numbers are posted for all to see and scrutinize.

Now, you might think that we were able to hit all of these amazing targets because we were flying a lot of new airplanes. We do keep our cabins very fresh and do a lot of modifications to our fleet to give that "new car" feel. The truth is that Richard Anderson had never met an old airplane that he didn't love, which meant we still were flying some old Douglas DC-9-51s up until 2014, even though they hadn't been in production since 1975! We were outperforming all of the other airlines in the world with airplanes that were far older—in other words, we had the oldest, but most reliable major commercial fleet in the world. Heck, the word "outperform" isn't even fair. We literally had more cancel-free days in some of these years than the rest of the industry combined. We weren't even in the same universe!

Goals are very powerful. You can't have the right goals without vision, and you can't share your vision without selecting the right style, if you want people to internalize it. But without goals, you cannot lead an industry. With the right goals that align with your vision and style, you can go places that nobody else can even dream of.

C.E. Woolman understood the necessity of constantly adapting to meet the ever-changing landscape of commercial aviation: "The only monotonous thing about the aviation industry is the constant change." And change it does. If you fail to change along with it, you will be left in the dust.

CHAPTER 4

Do Not Plan to Fail

Running an airline is like having a baby: fun to conceive, but hell to deliver.
–C.E. Woolman

Shortly after my wife, Catherine, and I got married, we did the next logical thing: we decided to buy a house. We made an agreement with each other that this was going to be our "forever house." Both of us really hated moving. So, we did the next logical thing after that: we bought an ugly house that needed a whole lot of work. We figured that if we were never going to move again, we'd get a place that we could afford, tear down the inside room by room, and build it back up the way we wanted it.

On March 1, 2004, we got the deed to our new home and, without any plan whatsoever, we went out and bought some critical supplies we thought would be good to have on hand: two crowbars, a trash can, and a sledgehammer. We got to work that day tearing apart our new home. Catherine started with the carpet. By the time I got home from work that first day of home ownership, half of our living room was a construction zone. We were staring at plywood subfloors by the end of day one. Success! This little project was already beginning to show visible results. Soon we'd transform that pet-stained, wall-to-wall carpeting with luxurious hardwood floors. Then we'd give the kitchen a face-lift. And after that, onward to the bedrooms, the bathrooms, and the sunroom. Last, but not least, we'd finish our basement, which was completely open and unframed. Maybe I'd even build out a little home theater, for old times' sake. We gave ourselves a ten-year goal to finish all of this. We estimated that we had plenty of time.

Three-and-a-half years into our project, that sledgehammer had gotten some pretty good use. We found ourselves a couple months away from our first child's due date, and we still hadn't finished the master bedroom. We had managed to refinish the kitchen, the dining room, and several other rooms, but we were running against the clock now if we wanted to have a room to move into when the baby arrived. We were living in the nursery, so that wasn't going to work. I sped up my pace a bit, buckling down in the last month. I laid more flooring, painted the walls, installed the crown molding, hung up a new ceiling fan, and, finally, brought in the master bedroom furniture that we'd been moving into different rooms around the house[14].

14 Which included the sunroom, where we had lived for the first two years. My wife is a very patient woman.

By the time our son, Charlie, was born, in June of 2007, I had managed to get the upper floor of our house nearly all finished. All that was left was to trade out some carpet in the sunroom for some travertine tile and build out our master bathroom, which was all bare studs and subfloor. There was no toilet, no sink/vanity, no running water, no tub, and no shower. I had used that sledgehammer, crowbar, and trash can to great effect in there. There was no need for us to rush to finish up the master bathroom, at the time, so we saved that project for another day. Our life was about to have a new focus, anyway, as our little baby boy was bouncing into our lives. And Catherine was still finishing up her master's degree in computer science. We still had no real concrete plan to finish the rest of the house.

A few years later, as the holiday season was approaching in 2010, home loan interest rates were plummeting. We thought it would be a good idea to refinance the house and maybe even take a little bit of cash out for a rainy day. We also wanted to roll in the home equity line of credit we took out to get our basement framed out, dry walled, and rough plumbed. With Charlie now three years old and his sister, Evelyn, fourteen months old, we'd given in and decided to get some contracted help here and there with the house. It was a project that was progressing slowly now that we had two little rug rats to chase around. The sunroom did get finished up, but I still hadn't tackled the master bath.

Our bank came back to us and offered us a nice rate to refinance the house. All they needed to do was send over a home appraiser to walk through our house so they could make sure that the home value matched what they had estimated from neighboring comps. Right before Thanksgiving, a guy came by, took some pictures of the house, jotted down some notes, and wrote up a report to send to the bank. With that out of the way, I gathered up the family and threw us all on a standby listing to get on an airplane to California. We'd be spending the week out there visiting my parents, my brother's family, and my sister.

The day before Thanksgiving, I got a call from our bank. They wanted to schedule a date for our closing and wanted to see if we'd be available to meet with the lawyer just after the new year in January of 2011. I didn't see any problem with that. But they did have one problem. They told me they had noticed that we had an unfinished master bathroom and that it would need to be addressed and reappraised no later than December 23rd or we'd lose the rate we wanted and would have to start the refinance process all over again. My heart sank for a moment, but then, after a couple seconds, I told the lady from the bank, "Sure thing. We'll take care of it. Go ahead and send the appraiser back over on the 23rd." The lady asked me if I was sure. I reassured her that I was.

My turkey dinner wasn't sitting as well as it might have in my belly the next day. My brain kept tumbling ideas around for somehow reassembling our master bathroom, in less than a month—during the holiday season, no less. Technically, I had everything I needed. I had all the tools, the equipment, the fixtures, and the know-how to get it all done. I just didn't know if I had the time to do it. So, I started to do what I always do when I get overwhelmed. I wrote down everything that I needed to do, in the order I knew I needed to get it done. And then I felt even sicker. There was such a lot to do.

I needed to frame out a new shower and bathtub surround. Plumbing needed to be rerouted for a new sink/vanity area. The toilet needed to be moved six inches from the wall (more of a pain in the butt than you might think, by the way). There was dry rot in the subfloor that needed to be addressed. The floor needed tiling. All of the electrical boxes needed to be moved or redone. New sheetrock needed to be hung, mudded, and painted. The shower needed a custom shower pan built, by hand (which I'd never done). And hundreds of pounds of mortar, travertine, and grout needed to be mixed, cut, and troweled in place. At the end, I would need to prove to the appraiser that everything was functional and in a sellable condition. It was clear that it was time for me to sit down and write up a plan to get this done.

Catherine and I looked at every available hour that we'd have in the next month to work on getting this laundry list of chores done, also bearing in mind that we had two very young children to feed, clean, entertain, and take to and from preschool. I was working full time, and Catherine worked 20 hours a week at Georgia Tech, so realistically, the hours of the day that we had available, aside from the weekends, were between about 6 p.m. and 2 a.m. for me and from about 9 p.m. to 2 a.m. for Catherine. Sometime during that window, we were going to have to get ready for Christmas as well!

We filled in every hour of every day that we had with the tasks that needed to get done, including the holiday prep. I looked at the timeline, and it just wasn't going to cut it. I needed to outsource a couple of the things on the list if I was going to make a December 23 appraisal. I decided to offload the shower pan, which I'd never done before, and the drywall installation and joint compound application, which I hated doing anyway. I persuaded a couple of contractors I'd used before to agree to come in at short notice; then I looked at my plan again and realized that we might just finish on time.

With everything now written down, down to the nitty-gritty detail, on exactly what we needed to accomplish each day, I felt a lot better about meeting the goal. I felt like the hard part was over, which was thinking things through and coming up with the plan itself. Now, all we had to do was the work we had written down.

The power of having a to-do list is pretty awesome. Once you break down a seriously complicated project into individual tasks and create a timeline for doing them all, you see how basic each task really is. Anyone that can operate a hand-held power drill, a basic chop saw, a tile cutter, and a jig saw can do everything we did during that month. Catherine took on the role of tile cutter, chop saw operator, and head of quality control. I operated the jig saw and power drill and provided the manual labor, which my back still complains about to this day. The rest was just about time, elbow grease, and sleep deprivation.

As we progressed through the month, I found, especially on the weekends, that we were getting ahead of schedule and could relax a little bit, here and there. We had our plan, and it was working. The detailed plan helped us to see what we needed to prep for the next day, and it set our expectations for ourselves every day. I knew if we had had a good day or a bad day by seeing what we had crossed off our to-do list. So, as December 23 approached, I felt pretty good about hitting our goal.

The home appraiser came in, as scheduled. I hadn't actually tested the shower yet, but we had everything hooked up and ready to go, should he ask to see it run. He didn't. He took some photos of the bathroom for his files to update the bank and left almost as quickly as he came. We'd made it on time! It didn't quite sink in that we were two days away from Christmas, but I was finally in the Christmas spirit.

I celebrated that next week by going over to my in-laws' house and retiling their bathroom floor. I know!

For anything that you're attempting to get done in life—and it doesn't matter whether it's in the business world, your home world, something you're volunteering to do in the community, or for your place of worship—if you've got a goal but no plan, then what you've done is you've *planned* to fail. Don't do this. You had such a great vision, your people genuinely like you because you used style to get them on board with that vision. Then, you worked with them to figure out good, measurable goals. Now, all you had to do was just sit down with your team and write down how you were going to hit those goals you came up with, together. That's where a plan comes in.

A goal is something that you can measure, but it is not a plan on how to reach the goal. You need a plan so you can answer the question, "Am I on track to meet my goal?" Everyone needs plans. Your company needs one at a very high level, your boss needs one for you and your peers to be successful, and you need one for each of your team members. If you are a frontline employee who is trying to hone in on your skills to get into a leadership role, then you can practice your planning skills in your work life or your personal life. It's the same skill you are developing, regardless of where you put it into play.

If you are leading a team, make sure that your planning activities are collaborative, even if it is a team in which none of the team members report to you (which is often the case, even when you get to relatively high levels of management). The plans that actually work are the ones where people get together, and you ask the question, "How are we going to reach our goal, together?" What you'll quickly find is, if you've invited all the right stakeholders to your planning session, people will actually volunteer their ideas on how to best hit the target. You don't even have to be very good at coming up with ideas—the team will do it for you.

If you are a new leader, it can be really difficult to let other people around you share their ideas. It can be tempting to think of yourself as the one who needs to dictate the plan. My advice, based on doing it this way too many times, is to shut up for a minute, and let the people you've surrounded yourself with answer the question. Your job is to facilitate, not to dictate. Leaders are people who allow the exceptional people they've hired to do their job and come up with ideas for how things should get done.

Employees who are good at their jobs generally know how things need to get done and the order in which those things need to happen. If step number one is to gather people who are good at their job together, step number two is to stop talking and listen to them tell you how to use those skills to get to the goal. During this step, just take a marker and walk over to your whiteboard and start writing down the things that come out of their mouths.

A lot of people will tell you to take the date you set as a goal to have something completed and work your way backward to create a plan that will fit inside the window of time you laid out before you started working out your plan and knew if you could hit that deadline. I'm going to buck that trend and tell you that I think this is absolutely wrong. The intent is understandable, but there's a better way to get to the date you want than to make everyone shoehorn in some unrealistic plan to make the boss or customer happy. People are good at telling you what you want to hear. But they'll do it at the expense of reality all day long.

I prefer to wipe the slate clean and take what I know to be the goal for completion and forget about it until my initial plan is completely drafted. This gets rid of any reason for people to try to give you their best-case scenario response for everything. I don't want *best* case. I want to know what is *real* case. Never plan on best-case scenarios. They never work, and when they start to fail, it just demoralizes the team, and you end up getting so far off track that your plan starts to not mean anything to anyone anymore. And I promise you this—if your plan starts to have no meaning, then you have no plan. And if you have no plan, you will fail.

With a clean slate, make your best attempt to chronologically lay out all the things that need to happen to get to your goal. Don't worry about missing a few details. You'll refine your plan as you go. At the start, it's just important that you hit the major steps that need to get done. Even more importantly, you need to identify *who* is responsible for accomplishing each of those major steps. (That will be the person who will need to make a more detailed plan with you later on). Fight the temptation to volunteer yourself to be one of these people. If you're a new leader, it's really tough not to volunteer to help—but you need the team to sign up for these responsibilities. Remember, you are tasked with leading the team. You were not hired to be the one doing the work.

You also need to understand how long each of those major steps are going to take. When you complete this first, simplified plan, you can take a look at the completion dates and see if they align with your goal. If they do line up, then you can be a little more confident that your original goal was pretty realistic, and now you've had your team give you an unbiased estimate to make you feel more confident about your ability to hit your goal date. If you started out by giving them the target ahead of time, you'd have missed out on that reassurance. If the rough plan you've just constructed *doesn't* meet your goals, that is the moment to go back and ask questions about how you can improve the dates.

One of the best benefits of having someone who is a good leader of people but not a subject matter expert leading a team is that those people will ask dumb questions that nobody would ask if they had done the job in a prior life. As a leader, one of your most powerful tools is asking dumb questions. The dumber you allow yourself to be, the more likely you are to accidentally stumble onto the right question that nobody else would think of asking.

Sometimes just asking one unintelligent question is the difference between signing up to do something totally impossible and recognizing it is impossible ahead of time and going back to ask your customer if they can change the requirements so you can succeed. Your customer will appreciate it if you do that ahead of time instead of mid-program. That is, after all, why they hired you. They trust you to be smarter than they are about the thing they hired you to do. Otherwise, they'd be doing it themselves.

There's always some wiggle room for you to adjust a plan that won't get to the target date that was given to you by your customer. When you ask your team members to give you standard completion times, for example, they shouldn't give you a plan that is going to require people to work overtime or come in on the weekends or adopt abnormal procedures to make a timeline work. If you end up needing to use a few of these Get Out of Jail Free cards to meet the goal, that's perfectly fine for short sprints. Just don't plan to do that over too long a time period. That isn't a good long-term plan to keep good people working for you.

Similarly, if you need to bring in a crew of contractors for six months to give you a labor boost because there's no way you can hit your goal with your current staff, that's another place where you can bend the rules to meet a tight deadline (as I did with my master bathroom.) If your company can afford to make those adjustments and the goal is that important, hiring contractors may be completely appropriate. But you only want to start thinking like that if your original plan, based on standard timelines, can't get you to your goal.

With each major step that your team identifies, you've also got to ask, "What are all the things that can go wrong?" Plan on a large percentage of things going wrong because they will. There are lots of models out there that recommend how much of a buffer to build into your schedule based on this. Find one that makes sense to you. But in short, you do need to know what can go wrong at each step and map out what the team would need to do to get back on track if those things happened and then built that into your plan. If you don't plan for mistakes, you are planning to fail.

Never plan to fail!

Next, you need to get buy-in from everyone around the table on your plan. This is a crucial step. To that end, you need to get good at recognizing if someone is going to pocket-veto the plan after they leave the room and figuring out how to get those people to buy into the plan. You need to ensure that when you all walk away, everyone is willing to get to the finish line together. If even one member of the team thinks that your plan is bad, that's a risk that you can't take, especially if that person is critical to making your plan succeed.

Having a basic plan where everyone knows what their role is, the timelines make sense to everyone, and the major risks are all identified ahead of time, gives you a good shot at hitting your goal. You have to deal with those basic things at the very beginning. I've seen cases where all of these things were done right and things that had seemed really hard turned out to be really easy to manage. But in cases when people don't understand the importance of doing all these things, I've literally seen companies go out of business as a result.

Having a good plan keeps you in business.

Late in 2018, I was approached by Rick Salanitri, president of DFP (my ultimate boss), about the idea of us taking on a big manufacturing project. Delta Air Lines had been working with a small company in Auburn, Washington, called TTF Aerospace, Inc. Delta had hired TTF to design and build a crew rest module, essentially a lower-deck cargo container, for their A330-900 Neo fleet. TTF, who had been struggling to stay in business for the previous few years, were close to being able to certify the module for this new fleet type, but they were going to need some major help building enough units to meet Delta's delivery plan.

TTF was a distressed company, and the only thing keeping them afloat was Delta fronting them cash and parts to keep their manufacturing line moving. This had been going on for several years. Rick asked what I thought about building the modules at DFP. I asked him if he wanted us to stay in business or not. He said he did. So, I told him that I thought it was a terrible idea.

To elaborate, a crew rest module is a full-width, lower-deck cargo container that is installed in the belly of a wide-body aircraft. It is outfitted with bunk beds, a heating system, lights, a reading chair, and a stairway that leads to a small hatch in the main cabin. It is designed to meet the resting requirements for flight crews doing long-haul[15] flights. These modules allow pilots and flight attendants to rest and sleep while a separate crew is operating the aircraft.

Long-haul flights require multiple crews to be on board so the crews can switch mid-flight, and the crew that started the flight can go to the crew rest area for some R&R. Whether or not they actually sleep while they are down there is up to them. But, you have to give them the facilities to bunk, and those facilities have to meet certain requirements for comfort so that the crews can be rested and ready to take over on the next shift somewhere 30,000 feet over the Pacific Ocean.

TTF Aerospace specialized in the design and manufacture of these complicated tree houses. We did not. They were hanging onto the last threads of solvency. I didn't want to end up suffering the same fate. Naturally, our president agreed to do the project. In reality, we never really had a choice. Someone had to come in and take on the task of building these things.

If TTF went under, Delta's brand-new A330-900 Neo fleet would essentially be worthless for international flying. It wouldn't do a lot of good to get these beautiful new airplanes and then be restricted to flying them from Seattle to Atlanta. They were meant to go from Atlanta to Tokyo, from New York

---

15 Reference 14 CFR 17 and FA Advisory Circular 117.1

to Seoul, or Los Angeles to Sydney. That's where we needed the long-range lift.

Our mission at DFP was to take on all of the high-risk projects that Delta needed to keep close to the vest. We weren't going to fail where other companies failed because we were the best people in the industry, handpicked to bring superior solutions to the airlines. Even though we were not crew rest manufacturing experts, we knew the fundamentals for building plans for just about anything. It was all about the process of getting from point A to point B. We'd done it with Wireless IFE, and now we were going to do it again with crew rests.

We had a really good project manager named Anne Carobine. She had been successful in getting our first program out the door and on time back in 2017 (the 777-200 mid-life mod). She had taken some important lessons that she had learned from the 777 program and now she injected them into the crew rest project. She learned that it was important to establish, at the outset, a core group of experts that we called an Integrated Product Team (IPT).

The IPT consisted of a program planner (from Supply Chain), a production planner (who planned the work on the floor), a manufacturing engineer (who designed the step-by-step methods to build the unit), a production supervisor (who oversaw the work on the floor), a quality engineer (who would be building in the inspection points during the manufacture), and a design engineer (who would field any requests for design changes along the way).

The company's goal was to deliver the first unit to Delta by the end of the calendar year in 2019. Anne's job was to project manage a plan to make this happen. She had the team create a full list of everything that had to get done to successfully deliver on time. Admittedly, the team didn't think of absolutely everything that needed to be done on day one, but they gave her enough of an idea of what needed to be done to draw up a rough schedule. More importantly, the plan showed that we might have some risks with the final acceptance testing being done before year-end; so we knew, way ahead of time, that we needed to tell Delta they'd need to do whatever it took to help TTF get as many units built as possible in 2019.

The IPT met every week, from the spring of 2019 to the delivery of the first unit. Each week, they followed up with each other on the status of each of the tasks that they assigned to each other the week before. For the most part, upper management was not involved in the week-to-week management of the project. There were issues that came up here and there, and the team came to us when they needed help with creating new processes or straightening out issues with suppliers, but for the most part, the team just took care of business week in and week out.

The sign of having a good plan in place is when you can completely step away and let the team take care of their issues as they keep marching toward the goal and clearing milestones. If this happens, don't step in and mess with it. You've hired people that you trust, and you hired them to work without you getting in the way and messing up everything. You do need to stay engaged with the team but only by asking intelligent questions about their progress.

For example, if you hear the supervisor volunteer the idea that they can make up some lost time in the upcoming week, you might ask them if they've considered the fact that there is a major holiday coming up next week. Or you might hear someone planning on mitigating a vendor delay by bringing the work in-house that the vendor was going to do. You may want to ask them if they have cleared material availability with the Supply Chain group or if the master scheduler is aware of this plan and can support with manufacturing labor and engineering. But, again, if the plan is good and is going smoothly, you shouldn't feel the need to invent problems to solve, so step away from the team and let them run it! That's why you hired them.

One of the most pleasing things I ever saw during my whole career at Delta and DFP was right before the big bonding event for the first crew rest build. Paul Polston, our production supervisor, who had been a career Boeing manufacturing guy before he came to DFP, was orchestrating a pre-bond preparation with the team. The crew rest module is, first and foremost, a three-dimensional jigsaw puzzle full of fiberglass-reinforced, flat honeycomb panels that are joined together with epoxy adhesive packed into hundreds of mortise-and-tenon joints. I watched as Paul had his team of technicians (mostly contractors) do various dry-fit attempts at putting the module together. Basically, you simulate bonding all of the pieces together, but you leave out the glue.

The team had a wall-mounted stopwatch timing their dry runs. After each run, the team stopped the time and talked about how they were going to improve on the next dry run.

Your epoxy adhesive only has a sixty-minute working life. That means that if you take longer than sixty minutes to apply the adhesive and fit everything together, you're going to have a big mess, and you might even be scrapping out a hundred thousand dollars' worth of panels and raw materials.

Paul had his team organized like a pit crew after the first few attempts. Even better, they went from over an hour for the first couple runs down to less than twenty minutes. When they completed their last dry run, the team was justifiably proud of the way they had worked together. It wasn't just the technicians there, though. One of the benefits of the Delta shops is that they're all non-union. That means the planners, QA guys, MEs, and design engineers could all grab their blue jeans and steel-toed shoes and go out and help on the floor without the fear of having a grievance filed against them. And they were all out there, strategically discussing and pantomiming each movement that the team needed to make to put the puzzle together cleanly so that when they did it with the epoxy all buttered into the mortises, it would be a clean build.

Each technician had specific panels (or puzzle pieces) assigned to them. And they had determined the exact order in which everything went together so when they practiced the movements together, it was seamless. In the end, it was like a synchronized ballet of honeycomb, rubber mallets, and glue. When they did it for real, everything went together so smoothly, not even a single joint needed to be repaired. Our first crew rest module actually started to look like a little house instead of a pile of flat pre-cut panels. It was a wonderful sight.

The team ended up having some issues, as anticipated, with the acceptance tester. TTF hadn't had the time to finish documenting how they had built their testing machine. I visited their plant in Auburn and asked their engineers some questions about how to replicate their tester: they explained that the drawings might or might not reflect what they actually built. It was on their to-do list to fix, but they had bigger fish to fry at that time. The tester was a bit of a Frankenstein device. It had clearly been designed as it was getting built. This isn't unusual in our industry, but it was a risk to the program that we needed to deal with.

Our concerns over the reproducibility of the TTF tester deepened late in December at DFP. To complicate matters, TTF had closed their doors at this point, so there wasn't going to be any help from the team who had been working there. But the DFP team fought through the holidays, getting a plan together to build it right (and documenting it with drawings that were accurate). The tester delay pushed the delivery of our first unit into early 2020, but because of the advanced warning we had given our customer early on, Delta had been able to push TTF to build one more unit than they had originally planned; the new schedule meant that we still had a good amount of buffer.

As luck would have it, the last TTF unit produced had issues during the installation in the hangar, but ours was ready earlier than we had promised to Delta; as a result, the first one we built was used in place of one of the last units built by TFF because of an installation issue Delta had with that last TTF unit. It was a big win for the team. Again, Rick was proven right for having challenged us to take on a risky program.

I was still learning the lesson that you just have to trust the DFP team to get it done! But getting it done means you must start with a good plan and execute it—as a team. And that's exactly what the team did.

Companies need plans, just like individual teams and projects need plans. At Delta, it is widely publicized that we have a Flight Plan that gets published for each calendar year. Richard Anderson initiated this during his time as CEO of Delta. The Delta Flight Plan includes a combination of visions, goals, and actual plans. It does a really nice job of establishing the annual targets for what we're supposed to focus on achieving, year-to-year, along with a little roadmap to help us achieve it.

It became pretty clear to all of us, very quickly, that our divisional goals would focus on a half dozen of these company-wide Flight Plan goals. Our job, at the mid-level management level, was to create a team plan for how to achieve each of these items. You did *not* want to be connected to any Flight Plan goal that didn't get met. That was a really big deal, and a potentially career-limiting (or ending) move, if you were the reason the company was unable to tick off that box at the end of the year.

But the amazing thing is that people are really good at doing things that you ask them to achieve, especially when you write those things down for them to see. Teams easily rally around clear plans. Ultimately, people want to do a good job, and when they go home at the end of the day, they want to know that they did what they were supposed to do. It's a strange and even depressing feeling to go home and not have any idea if what you did mattered or if your work was useful to anyone. If what you did was a documented task on a plan that you are a part of, it's easy to point to that thing and get satisfaction from your accomplishment. Generally, people get satisfaction from being able to put a checkmark next to a completed task. It almost doesn't matter what that task is.

We are just programmed to love crossing stuff off to-do lists.

At the end-of-year review at the leadership conference held in Atlanta each year right around bonus season, which falls on Valentine's Day), we always review how we did with last year's Flight Plan. One of our favorite things to do is to review all the items on the plan and then see all the things that got a green check mark next to them. Year-in and year-out, we hit 85-90% of them all. And they're not easy goals: "Become the industry leader in on-time departures"; "Increase Delta's industry lead by 10% in Net Promoter Score"; or "Increase past last year's record profits by 20%."

It's amazing the progress you can make as a company with a simple plan. You can even achieve things you were convinced were impossible before you broke it down into bite-size pieces.

CHAPTER 5

Communicating Expectations

The character of our company... it's not me... it's US. You are the character of this company... every one of you. Character isn't just being nice to people. Character is being efficient; character is being productive.
–C.E. Woolman

Sometime after Delta merged with Northwest Airlines, I took on my first position as a manager with direct reports in the engineering department. I was given a rebuilding task of sorts. There was a small group of operations engineers in Atlanta and a handful more in Minneapolis that effectively had no direct manager until I came to the team. Airline experts are subdivided into what we call Air Transport Association (ATA) chapter codes. We were the operations team that handled ATA 25, which is cabin interiors. My job title was Cabin Operations Engineering Manager."

The Atlanta Cabin Ops group had a lead engineer, Gary "Tabb" Pearson, who had effectively been in charge of the day-to-day operations until I got there. We had both applied for the job that I took, but later on he told me that he hadn't really wanted to take on the management role. For him, it would not have been a pay grade change so there wasn't any pay incentive for him. He was already at the top of his pay scale on the technical track, which was equivalent to the manager pay grade I hired into. I knew that Tabb had applied for my role, so when I started, I made sure that I sat down with him first, before I sat down with anyone else on the team. It was important to get his insight as the resident lead of the team.

Tabb had been burning the candle at both ends of the wick for some time. He was tired and had been working hard. I think he had applied to the manager position out of a sense of obligation more than a sense of wanting the role. He told me he had been somewhat relieved when he found out that I had accepted the job. I think it took a little weight off of his shoulders to have someone else come in, to add another body to throw at the work[16]. They were overwhelmed by a growing fleet with growing needs, a merger that was sucking up a lot of their time, and the group had not grown in head count

16 Tabb actually did eventually take a manager role in this group after I left, and it was at a time when he truly wanted it. The group grew so large that the position I was in had to be elevated to a general manager role and Tabb became one of three managers that would ultimately report to that new GM position. The Cabin Ops manager position I held was one of two front-line manager positions that I served in that eventually got upgraded to GM positions after I left them.

over the previous years as the workload had increased. In many ways, there was a still a pre-bankruptcy mindset in that group.

It was pretty natural for Tabb to put in ten-, eleven-, or twelve-hour days, as he had been working so hard. It was eight at night when we wrapped up our first conversation. Naturally, he looked at the other people on his team and had some issues with a couple of the engineers who weren't putting the same kind of effort as him. There was one employee in particular that he mentioned who, in his estimation, just was not putting in an acceptable level effort. I'll call this guy Tim.

Tabb gave me a lot of detail on Tim's shortcomings. He arrived, typically, after 9 a.m, while the rest of the team got to work before 8:30. He would routinely leave before 5 p.m. His workload also wasn't as big as the others on the team. Tim never asked Tabb if he could take anything off anyone else's plate, either. He just did his own thing and didn't seem to be taking a fair share of the team's load. I thanked Tabb for telling me this and promised him that I would keep an eye on Tim.

My new boss, Ana Tharp[17], sat me down the next day, my first official day on the job, and relayed the same concerns to me. She pointed out to me how hard Tabb had been working, which was already obvious. And she really was upset that another team member could have the gall to be taking advantage of the company. I already knew that one of her pet peeves was people taking advantage of the company's flexibility, including being

17 Ana was the first Delta leader who took a chance on me to lead a team. I learned a lot from her about how I needed to behave as a leader. Most importantly, I credit her with teaching me how to think before I speak – something I didn't do very well before I worked with her.

trusted to arrive and leave at the right time and not properly recording vacation and time-off. The first mission that she gave me was to observe Tim closely and to consider putting him on a performance improvement plan (PIP).

Now, if you've never heard the term, PIP is often synonymous with "you're about to get fired." At least, that's how a lot of companies approach PIPs. A PIP is accompanied by a formal "last warning" letter that is issued to the employee that basically says that one wrong move and you'll be considered for termination. Attached to the letter is a "plan" that the employee has to follow in order to get back into good standing.

The standard industry practice is to structure the improvement plan in a way that is so challenging that you know the employee will fail if they don't significantly change their ways. By the time someone has been given a PIP, you're usually looking for a way to show them the exit. However, to be fair, you have to give them a chance to prove themselves should they choose to put in the effort to save their job. Across all industries, about 80%[18] of all employees that go on a PIP fail and get terminated.

Knowing that I was on a mission to find and document every last fault that I could find with this Tim guy, I went out of my way during the first few weeks on the job to collect first-hand evidence of his performance. One of the first things I sent out to the whole group was a decree that everyone was required to come to work no later than 8:30 each morning. On top of that, everyone had to account for a minimum of one

---

18 I make up about 65 percent of all of the statistics I reference in this book.

hour for lunch, and everyone had to put in a full eight hours per day of working time, without exception. And if anyone had any issues with this, they needed to come to me.

I got exactly one reply from my e-mail decree to the team. It was from Tim. He replied, "No problem. I'll see you at 8:30." That was it. Well, okay. That was easy. This whole manager thing was starting to feel good. People were starting to obey my authority. Now what was I supposed to do?

I started to look for some extra things that I could give Tim to do. I had just been given a really tedious task from our director of engineering that I wasn't really interested in doing myself. As a part of the merger with Northwest Airlines, we had to merge our records of the FAA-mandated Engineering Orders (EOs) for our fleet into the computer program we had inherited from Northwest Airlines, which was called SCEPTRE. All of the pre-merger Delta Air Lines EOs had to be converted over to the SCEPTRE format, which was a big pain in the butt. This stack of papers on my desk that was over two feet tall had Tim's name all over it.

I invited him into my office and handed over this huge stack of paperwork and told him what I needed him to do. I gave him a rough date for when I expected him to get done with it, and he didn't protest one bit. He said that he was really excited to get to know SCEPTRE better, and that this would give him a great opportunity to learn it. Somewhat taken aback, I sent him on his way and thanked him for his willingness. Everyone else I'd ever talked with from the pre-merger Delta side hated the idea of learning SCEPTRE (including me).

Tim came back into my office a couple days later, gave me about a quarter of the stack I had given him back and told me I could take those off the list because they had been erroneously included in the list of mandatory EOs, as they were not FAA-required at all. Soon after, he returned another stack to me and said he had finished his task on those and was starting to figure out the SCEPTRE system a little better. I went through his work and double checked it. I found a couple of minor issues, but nothing to write home about. I turned in half the stack I had been given to the chief engineer and tried to come up with some more things I could assign to Tim. I got him a couple more things to load him up on, and over the next couple weeks, he finished up everything I gave him.

Next came one of the most awkward meetings I've ever had to have with an employee. My general manager reminded me that we still needed to sit down with Tim and go over his year-end performance, which I had already been told was going to result with him being issued with a PIP and giving up the pay raise that the rest of the employees across Delta were going to get that year. I told Ana about my recent experiences with Tim and how he'd really done quite well taking direction from me and was doing the tasks I gave him in less time than I had expected. I also mentioned that the quality of work was reasonably high.

Ana thought for a split second and then a look of clarity came across her face as she told me that he was, no doubt, trying to make a good impression, knowing that he had been given a poor performance review by his previous boss. The past review had been given by the previous GM prior to her coming on board about a month before I got there. I didn't think to ask her for a copy of the review to read. I figured she'd read it already, and I generally trusted her because of her reputation for being attentive to detail. Plus, I had already learned to trust her gut with personnel issues from working with her in the past, so I went along with it, reinvigorated with the idea that we were about to do the right thing. So, we decided to bite the bullet and have the tough conversation with Tim, together, right then and there.

Tim came into the office and sat down beside me. I shot him a sheepish look as my boss introduced the reason we were all there. He listened, with a shocked look on his face when he realized he was being told that he was one false step away from being fired from the company. When Ana finished her litany of things that we had against him, including his written performance review from the previous general manager, he just sat there with a look on his face like he'd just been ambushed.

A couple of seconds went by, then he looked at me. I admit I felt a little bit like he was going to say to me, "Et tu, Brute?" I could almost see a knife with my initials lodged squarely in his back. What he actually said was, "I actually thought I was going to talk to you two today about getting promoted to senior engineer." He had had no idea that anyone ever thought he was underperforming. In fact, he and his wife had been talking about starting a family, and he was hoping that he would sit down with us and go over the next steps to get a pay increase so they could afford to do that. They had just bought a house—actually in the same general neighborhood that my wife and I were raising our young family at the time.

Being the focused leader Ana was, she quickly went into the system and pulled up his previous performance review: she remembered the previous GM had put in some written notes that would support the history of poor performance. She printed it out and we looked at it together. Tim looked at it. I looked at it. And he looked at us and asked where in that review was his performance listed as subpar. I was about to ask the same thing, but I held back. Ana pointed out where her predecessor wrote about some things that Tim should do for improvement, which included looking for ways to take on more work to help out the team.

To be fair, every year in every employee's performance review, there is always a note in there about what we can do to improve. I think Ana and I saw very quickly, at the same time, how that may have been perceived by Tim during his read-through of his performance review. There's a difference between the message that there are somethings you can do to improve versus someone telling you, plainly, that you are on thin ice and if you don't improve, you'll be out the door. Maybe the previous GM hadn't had as tough of a talk as we had perceived he had. Ana was also relatively new to the group, so we were both going off the emotion of how the story was told to us by our respective predecessors. Apparently, things weren't as clearly communicated as we had believed.

I turned to Tim and told him that we would work together to create a fair plan and that we would sit down right away and talk in detail about the perceptions of his work ethic, his time away from the office, his perceived lack of willingness to step up to help the team who were all working hard, and so on. I gave him a reassuring look, and he gave me a resigned look that said, "Okay." Ana gave me a nod, and I went back to my office to sit down with my emotionally deflated engineer.

I closed the door when we got back to my office and invited Tim to sit down. The first thing I told him was that, from what I had seen during the past couple of weeks, if he continued to do the tasks I was assigning him, he would have no problem getting through the PIP. I reviewed the tasks I'd given him since I had started with the group and pointed out the good things I had seen him doing, and I also told that him that he was, by all appearances, honoring my request to get to work on time and staying for a full eight working hours.

I decided to confide in him a bit. I told him that I had seen that he seemed sincere when he said he had never had a conversation about any negative performance with either his lead, Tabb, or his previous GM. He reiterated to me that there had been no previous mention to him of anyone being upset with his performance. In fact, he had felt that the only role he had been given by his previous boss was to make sure he answered any questions from the configuration desk (Technical Publications) about which parts should be effective for the various pre-merger Delta fleets. This was something he felt he was particularly good at with his previous background with Fleet Engineering, where he had been before coming to the Cabin Ops team. He thought he was highly efficient with his job and that he gave good customer support. He said that even took his laptop home to finish up some tasks there when he could do so.

So, I asked Tim why he had a history of arriving to the office so late. He was a little taken aback at that question and told me that nobody had ever told him that starting after nine was a problem. That sounded fair, I supposed. But what about all those times when he had left early—before he completed a full eight hours of work? Tabb had kept a log of the past several months and he gave it to me, documenting Tim's arrival and departure times each day.

After Tim looked at the log I gave him to review that I had received from Tabb, he asked if he could go back to his desk really quick to get something. When he came back, he brought a printout of a log of vacation time that he had been keeping for the past year. When I married the two logs, they were a pretty close match. So, he had, indeed, been leaving early, but he had been using vacation time. Nobody had asked him about it. He had his vacation records fairly well in order, so we just came up with an agreement on how we were going to communicate that going forward.

In the end, we agreed to a three-month PIP where we'd monitor his arrivals and make sure we were communicating expectations for work assignments, and we both left the conversation feeling good about his chances of being successful with his plan.

What nobody had done, in any of the previous months, maybe years with Tim, was to sit down with him and go over basic expectations for what he was supposed to do, who he was supposed to report to day-to-day, and how to manage things like taking time off and getting work assignments.; he had just been doing whatever seemed logical to him. Because there were no daily team meetings, there was no way for him to see how busy everyone around him was or to talk about who needed help or who was open for taking on more work. He had had literally no idea that people resented him for not having as much work assigned to him as they did.

I went back and asked Tabb if he had ever sat down with Tim and gone over expectations. Tabb said he had understood that his old boss, Bill, had been doing that. Bill had actually retired from Delta, but he had come back as a contractor and was working as an engineer in the Liaison Engineering group. Ana tracked him down and asked him what he had told Tim. Bill said that they had kind of talked about him stepping up to take on more work, and he had thought that he had written something clear about that in his performance review before he retired. However, as Ana and I already figured out the hard way, he didn't quite write that review with the precision that he intended. In the end, Bill never clearly communicated anything in writing about what he expected from Tim or what the consequences might be if his performance didn't improve. I had assumed that this had already been communicated with him. Ana had assumed that Bill and Tabb had both done all this already. Tabb had assumed Bill had done it[19] and Bill had misremembered exactly what he had communicated to Tim when he handed over the reins to Ana. And for a guy who had a lot on his mind, with an imminent retirement, this isn't

---

19 After all, Tabb wasn't Tim's boss. It wouldn't really have even been appropriate for him to have that conversation with Tim as his technical lead.

exactly shocking. So that's how we got to the PIP discussion with such a shock to Tim.

Now, to support Ana's approach, she regularly used the PIP process as a tool to legitimately improve people's performance. I do remember several people who were not performing well underneath her where she used the PIP as an effective tool to get them to improve to the point where they were contributing to the team. She reminded me of these past successes and that Tim had also played a role in getting to where he ended up. She reminded me that communication is a two-way street, and he had not been pulling the weight that the others on the team had been pulling. I couldn't deny that as a clear fact. He probably ought to have recognized this on his own. Tabb wasn't wrong about that, and Tim hadn't really dug in to find out how he could help more. That was something that had been under his control, and he hadn't chosen to be the master of his fate. Ana was right to point this out and for pushing the tough conversations we had to have with Tim.

However, as it turned out, for the next year and a half that I led that team, I got nothing but positive work from Tim. He did everything I asked him to do. He became my resident expert on the new SCEPTRE system at a time when none of the pre-merger Delta engineers wanted to have anything to do with SCEPTRE. In fact, he set a company-wide record for the quickest project completion with the new system for all of Delta Engineering that first year using that old Northwest tracking system. I approved the work he did on that one, so I got to see first-hand that the quality was there, along with the speed.

Tim became one of the employees I could entirely rely on, for instance, to do emergency tasks and get involved with the cross-divisional projects that were still going on to finalize the merger. He even went on a last-minute rescue trip to Singapore for two weeks on zero notice to support a modification to our Boeing 747 fleet. He had become an expert on that project prior to that trip, and I needed someone out there to help get some work unstuck. So, he volunteered to go to help the team. I think I gave him a whole two hours to go home, pack, and then jump on a 747 departing from Atlanta to Narita, Japan so he could catch a flight to Singapore and help out the on-site team there for the next two weeks.

After simply sitting down with him and providing some detailed expectations, Tim became highly successful in getting his PIP completed satisfactorily. In fact, with a little politicking over the next year, I was able to put his name in front of the promotional review board, and before I left the group, I got him successfully promoted to Senior Engineer. He and his wife had a baby boy shortly after that, and I couldn't have been happier for them.

It can be difficult to effectively communicate expectations in the workplace, and there's always the possibility of miscommunication and assumption. We need to realize, as leaders, that the vast majority of employees want to do a good job. When people get clear instructions on what they need to do to please their boss, they typically do it, if they can.

Obviously, this story was a case study in what can happen if you fail to communicate expectations. Employees make assumptions about what "good" looks like. If their version of "good" doesn't match what their colleagues think, then they are perceived to be bad employees. Sometimes the difference between a "bad" employee and a useful team player is taking the time to sit down and go over what you expect. It can be that easy, and thankfully, it often is.

Communicating expectations becomes even more important on a grander scale. When you've got a really great idea and turn that idea into a vision, then develop a really effective way to relate that vision to other people, you can get some thoughtful feedback from your team on what your goals should be over certain periods of time. Once you've set your goals, you'll need to get together with your team to construct a plan. However, that's not the end of your responsibilities as a leader. Having a plan is of no use if you don't have a way to let everyone know what the plan is, and even more importantly, to make it clear what each person's *role* is in that plan.

Now, let's be really honest. When you make your plans, you don't always involve every member of your team in the early stages. To take it to an extreme, if a company like UPS had to involve all of their employees in every plan they made, they'd have over a million people in the planning room. There's no effective way to do that. You'd never make any decisions. But the plan that you make at a high level at a company like that absolutely has the potential to impact a million people. What you've got to figure out is how to effectively communicate the plan to all of those people who we call "stakeholders" (which just means anyone who is impacted by the plan, for better or for worse).

The stakeholders of your plans may be three to five people or there may be hundreds or thousands. The larger the number of stakeholders, the larger the communication campaign has to be to get the word out on what everyone needs to do to execute the plan successfully. You can't just sit in a room with a few leaders, come up with a plan, shake hands, and then expect that everyone who wasn't in that room magically knows what you discussed, right?

For me, this is actually the hardest part of leading people. Figuring out how to make sure everyone knows their role is difficult, even if you are dealing with small numbers of people. For example, I had to get a system in place quickly when I was leading a crew of engineers that did rotating shifts. I had six different shifts throughout the week, and whenever something changed about the process that we used (like our team's execution plan), I had to think about how I was going to make sure how the new expectations would be communicated to the crews that worked the weekends, the midnight shifts, and the evening shifts on both ends of the week when I would not be there to do the communicating.

That may sound like an extreme case, but it's really not. A lot of us have team members on the East Coast, the West Coast, out in Singapore, Europe, and so on. And we are getting a good taste during the pandemic of what the future will be like with more people working from home. So, we're recognizing the need to use technology to help us communicate. This means we all need to think hard about how to make our plans clear to our teams when we don't have the luxury of sitting in the same room to explain it to everyone face-to-face.

Here's something else I learned the hard way: you can't expect that hearing a plan once, even if you confirm everyone on your team heard and understood it, is enough for them to remember it well enough to implement it. Bear in mind that people take vacations and sick days. Was every stakeholder there on the day you gathered everyone together to tell them your plan? Who was missing that day? How will they get indoctrinated into the plan when they return?

Change management—which is dealing with any new thing, whether it be a new plan, a change of plans, a revision to a process, or a change to project requirements—is the single most difficult thing to implement successfully in any organization, no matter how big or small that change is. And that's effectively what communicating a plan is. It's managing change. Every new plan changes someone's job duties, and they will have to learn about, understand, and then put into practice these new duties before they get good at doing them.

If you had a group of youth basketball players, you wouldn't expect, on day one, your team of eight-year-olds to play flawlessly after going over the basics one time with them. Dribble the ball down the court. Avoid defenders along the way—but don't foul them. Remember not to double-dribble. Be careful not to travel. Don't go backward across the half-court line. Never stand in the key for longer than three seconds. No goaltending. Put the ball in the basket. Okay, team, you know the basics, now go play some basketball! We know that wouldn't work. You've got to drill each element into the team until they show understanding and then, after much practice, it becomes second nature.

In the same way, teams of adult coworkers need to be constantly coached so that everyone knows the plan well and so that, when people start exercising the plan, you can see if they understand it in the same way as the small team that drew it up with you. However, you don't want to nag your team. Coach them. Set the expectation for what everyone should be doing. This doesn't mean you need to micromanage them either.

In the last chapter, I talked about the crew rest module project that our team took on at DFP. The crew all knew the exact things that they needed to do because their supervisor took the time to explain the plan and make sure that everyone on the team knew what they were supposed to do. They were well coached, and the expectations were clear. That's one of the big reasons why they succeeded.

As a leader, your job is to make sure that you anticipate how every element of the plan is going to be understood by everyone who is involved in making that plan work. Remember that it only takes one person who doesn't understand their role for catastrophic failure to result. Take your time on this step. It's the most critical of them all. If you are going to spend extra time as a leader on any one of these principles, spend the most time on communicating expectations, especially expectations of people's role in carrying out an important plan. Decide ahead of time, with your team, on how the communication is going to happen. And make sure you do it frequently so that everyone gets to the point that they are tired of you communicating the plan. You cannot over-communicate the plan. Have I said that enough times? Communicate the plan!

To make sure you get regular opportunities to verify that everyone understands the plan and is implementing it correctly, take the time to schedule one-on-one meetings with each of the team members that directly report to you. You shouldn't go more than a couple weeks at a time without doing this, but you can do this as often as both of you need. Standardize what you talk about. At the very minimum, make sure the two of you agree on how to measure their progress on their portion of the overall plan. Talk about their progress every time you sit down with them. Then ask them what their roadblocks are to hitting each planned item.

You don't want to sign up to remove all of their roadblocks, but there will be some things that only you can resolve. Try to make it so you are telling them how to solve their problems, on their own, but offer to take on some actions yourself. Above all, write down every action item that the two of you talked about so that when you meet up the next time, you have a list of those things that each of you promised to do. This helps you keep each other honest, and it creates accountability in both directions. If you only do one thing, this is paramount. You will eliminate the kind of miscommunication situation that I walked into with my friend Tim.

The beauty of setting expectations and routinely following up and measuring performance of those expectations is that in the rare case where you have someone who consistently cannot complete the actions they signed up to do, it's really darned easy to tell when you need to use the performance improvement plan. In those cases, you've got to stick to your guns. When you get to that point, do not *ever* enable anyone to get off that PIP unless they absolutely nail the plan. If they do, then you've gained a valuable resource, like I did. If they don't (and I've had that happen too), then it's a lost cause, and it's best to end that cause sooner, rather than later.

In the late part of 2018, our little Delta Flight Products subsidiary was finally starting to get some sea legs and not a moment too soon. We were getting into the throws of production on our first large program where the majority of the products were being produced on-site in our factory. We were still growing rapidly as a company. We ended 2018 with an order backlog of $298 million. For a company of just over 200 employees, that's well over a million dollars in planned revenue for every single employee in the company. With commitments made and order books filled up, we had a huge need for developing effective ways to communicate our plans effectively to the employees that we were going to rely on to do the work.

We absolutely needed to start to get some of those 5S principles of Lean organizational management instituted at DFP. But we were still struggling to get out of "startup mode." Rick Salanitri had been handed a brochure by someone from one of the Georgia Tech affiliates we had been working with to develop our Wireless IFE product. It was for another group associated with them called the Georgia Manufacturing Extension Partnership (GaMEP). He tossed it on my desk and asked me to call them. They were supposed to be good at helping companies like ours begin their journey into Lean manufacturing. I was open to the idea, so I agreed. He warned me, though, that he'd spent hundreds of thousands of dollars in his career paying consultants to come in and try to implement Continuous Improvement programs. And most of the time, it had failed.

With that little pep talk out of the way, I still thought I'd give these GaMEP folks a call. I called them and got in touch with a guy named Larry Alford. Larry showed me some different things that his organization had done in working with local Georgia-based manufacturers, and he promised me two things—firstly, that his team would come in and show us ways to increase efficiency, and secondly, that it wouldn't cost a lot of money. That second one really hit a chord with me, so I invited Larry and the GaMEP team in for a two-day discovery engagement.

Larry came in with three specialists who each had a focus on different aspects of manufacturing, including design and project management. These were all things that we did at DFP. They asked me to create a schedule for them to be able to interview key people in the company who did everything from design engineering and project management to supply chain management, production planning, quality assurance, and information technology. They also asked me to schedule time with them to meet each of our senior leaders. So, I set up a two-day schedule for them to do some speed dating with all of these DFP specialists and senior leaders.

The GaMEP team asked each team member a few things. Their questions included asking what each person thought DFP was most in need of, what their biggest roadblocks were, and where the company most needed improvement. Based on our answers, the GaMEP team collected all of their interview notes, gathered together to share their notes with each other, and rounded all of the DFP leaders up for a close-out on day two.

Rick joined us for this. He was sitting right across the table from me. While we were waiting for everyone to finish lunch so the GaMEP team could start their close-out presentation, Rick told me that he would bet me a dollar that this engagement would be a complete failure and be a waste of our time and money. I took this as a personal attack on my ability to make this succeed, so in front of everyone in the room, I took his bet and told him he was going to lose. We shook hands, then Larry looked at me and asked me if we were ready. He gave me a little smile. I think he was glad I had taken that bet.

He launched into a summary of some of the most common things the DFP interviewees had pointed out to his team. One of the most amazing things that consultants do is take the things that you tell them and then put those things into a presentation, then tell you the things you should have already known, but don't. It's funny that so many people pay to have people come in and tell them what they should already know. But it's also funny that it's such a valuable thing to do.

Of the things that we had all told the GaMEP team—the one thing that stuck out the most—was that almost everyone they sat down with from the DFP team, including Rick, had said we had way too many meetings during the week. In fact, the number of meetings we were having was preventing us from being able to do the things that the meetings decided we should go and do. All we did, it seemed, was to go from meeting to meeting to meeting and then—poof—the day was over. We rinsed and repeated this process until the week was over.

This acknowledgement of our meeting-palooza problem was music to my ears. One thing you learn quickly when you get into Quality is that you're involved with just about everyone else's business—from Finance and Engineering to Production and Supply Chain. The Quality team gets sucked into all of it. Consequently, my day was all about meetings. It was really comforting to hear that everyone else felt the same way I did. We were all tired of the wall-to-wall meetings with which we had inflicted ourselves. We were a bit deflated when Larry told us that the solution to all of our meetings was to add another meeting to our day. I was feeling like a lonely little dollar bill was already starting to dislodge itself from my wallet. Oh well, at least these GaMEP guys were inexpensive.

But the next thing that Larry said was that by adding this one little meeting at the beginning of our day, we'd actually find that several other meetings would start to disappear from our calendars. Now this was something I could get behind. It didn't make a bit of sense to me, but at least I was listening.

The meeting they were describing sounded, actually, like it was more of a walk. They had named this daily walking meeting Managing for Daily Improvement (or MDI). In reality, what they were selling to us was the idea that we should implement something a lot of companies call a Gemba Walk. Gemba is an English transliteration of a Japanese word that just means "the actual place." If you are going on a Gemba Walk, you are walking to "the actual place" where things in your factory are having value added. Basically, you're getting out of your chair and you're walking to the place where things actually happen (which is never a meeting room).

Larry explained to us that we should really look at our manufacturing plant and start to figure out how the parts that are manufactured there flow through it. To do this, you start at the last step (the shipping department) and you trace your way back through the process, including all the shops (sheet metal fabrication, composite fabrication, machine shop, wire shop, and so on) all the way to the beginning of the manufacturing process (the raw materials receiving department). You set up stops along the way between these two points so that you go to all of the areas each day and talk with leaders who are supervising work in each of these areas.

The idea is that you take the management team, who need to understand the issues that the production floor has and help them understand these problems by going to "the actual place." It probably sounds better in Japanese than it does in English, hence the renaming to MDI. Nevertheless, in each of the places where you stop and talk with the employees who run that work cell (or an area in a Lean company organized around the production of a specific product or product group), you install a whiteboard with colored markers. The simple idea is that you write down what the problems are and then the management team figures out who is going to own finding the solution. Then everyone agrees on a due date to provide each solution. You write down the who, what, how, and when for each action.

The concept is truly simple, but you can supplement it to make it as sophisticated as you want. Or you can keep it simple. For example, on your whiteboard, you are encouraged to develop metrics that are important to each area and related to their goals, which they keep in their work cell. Ideally, you track two or three key metrics that are health indicators for that work cell. The rule is you have to track results every day. If the results show that the area didn't meet their goals, you talk about *why* the team hadn't been able to meet that goal. And, if something is preventing the team from being successful, someone from the management team needs to take an action, which gets written down on the board. You keep it up there until it gets done and confirmed by the local work cell leader.

The expectation you are communicating to everyone is that, while failures are going to happen from time to time, it's not okay to fail to take action when anyone on the team notices that there is a roadblock to success. And the other expectation that you are communicating to the whole team is *who* is expected to do *what* in order to remove that roadblock and by *when* they are expected to have it removed. The walk was a smart way for employees to communicate what they needed to finish a plan on time and for managers to communicate to those employees about how *they* planned to give their support to the team.

At first, we didn't feel comfortable with the process. We didn't really have any metrics for the production shops. Our production leaders wanted to delay rolling out this new MDI process until they could develop metrics. They asked when it would be a good time to roll out a process like this, given that we didn't even have established metrics for our shops yet.

One of the GaMEP team members, Mike Stonecipher, answered, "That's like asking, 'When do you want to start eating healthier?'" His point was that we shouldn't worry ourselves about shooting for perfection right away: we should just start the process and develop it as we go. If you don't have metrics, then at least get out on the floor and start talking with the machine operators and ask them, "What do you need us to do for you today?" They'll certainly start telling you. After all, they are the experts at the things that drive them nuts every day, especially when you're failing to provide for them.

As a leader, one of the most important things you can do is show up every day and set the expectation that you are going to be engaged in your team's business. Once they see that you are willing to go out to *their* office everyday, then they'll feel comfortable with sharing the things that cause them problems. These are actually the things that cause *you* problems without you even knowing about it until *they* tell you it's a problem for you. And, when they tell you about your team problems, you've got to write them down and then talk about it every day until it gets fixed.

We implemented MDI and quickly saw the importance of this process in our business. The guys on the shop floor may not have had any metrics to track early on, but they did know our business. In many ways, they knew it better than *we* knew it. When they started to trust us, they wrote down their problems and told us about them, thus communicating to us the problems they couldn't solve by themselves.

Some of the issues they brought to us were really simple things like not having enough aluminum plate on the floor to run a job that was hot. Then, the supply chain manager took the action to make sure more got ordered so that a job that had been stopped on the floor could finish up. That's not a hard thing to do, but the guys on the floor couldn't solve it on their own. They don't have access to their own buyers. They're busy running machines and making parts. When the management team got them the material they needed, they began to trust that they could bring bigger issues to us.

They started bringing more important problems to the MDI exercise. For instance, 20% of the aluminum parts that flowed through the manufacturing areas seemed to be getting damaged before they reached final inspection. That's a pretty big deal. We hadn't known that was happening. Maybe that had something to do with why we kept running out of that plate material! And shoot, that's something we need to track. There's a metric! Reduce the percentage of parts that run through the shop and get nicked, scratched, gouged, and scraped from 20% to a couple percent.

The parts receiving area leads and the wire shop leads were the first ones to figure out how to use metrics to their advantage. The receiving guys charted out how many items were getting blocked from being received because of missing paperwork from our vendors. They graphed the number of outstanding parts on the dock with missing paperwork. That created the expectation with the purchasing team that they needed to drive that number down and to work more closely setting expectations with our suppliers. The wire shop figured out they were having too many engineering design revisions. So, they started to plot out the daily open engineering errors. This made the management team focus in on all of the ways we could work to reduce the engineering design errors down to zero.

All the while, this little walk started a journey in continuously improving the life of the technicians on the floor, which led to efficiencies being gained and trust developed among the teams. Six months into our MDI exercise, we had meaningful metrics with goal rates established for every area within our production plant. People could plainly see, just by walking up to each work cell, if we had had a successful day or not. The expectations were becoming clear, and when you have clear expectations, the team can rally around fixing the issues that prevent "good" from happening.

All of us on the team were capable of going into any area in the building and explaining, in a ton of detail, the issues were we were trying to solve together. Do you think we eliminated some of our meetings? I can tell you, from my calendar, *I* certainly did. Over time, my mornings became much more streamlined. I got the important tactical decisions out of the way before 8:30 a.m., and the team had an agreed-upon direction coming out of that walk, every day. We knew what we had to do just by spending five minutes at each work cell talking with the local leader of that area and noting the actions we needed to take.

It got to the point where Rick would do tours of our building, and we'd see him walking around some VIP airline customers or walking his boss, Delta's COO, Gil West, through the building. He'd stop in front of one our whiteboards, and we'd see them pointing at charts showing metrics and goal lines that the shop technicians had come up with to track and solve our team problems.

I waited a full year. Rick never brought up our bet. One day, I heard him talking with one of our Airbus reps who was on site. He was mentioning how we have this great process for problem solving, and it was improving our employee engagement. He was bragging so much about this process that I felt it was time to collect. Later that day, I mentioned to him that I had overheard him.

Then I asked if he remembered our bet. Begrudgingly, he admitted that he did. And he sighed and gave me a coy little smile. He started to dig into his wallet to find a one-dollar bill. I stopped him. I already had a crisp, unfolded bill that was frame worthy, ready to go, so I handed it to him for him to sign.

In any case I think the whole bet was a setup from the beginning. He had known that, if he egged me on, I'd see to it that his money wouldn't get wasted. But I didn't care. He signed my dollar bill, and I won a bet. Today, it is one of my most treasured possessions. It says, "You were right. This time....", signed Rick Salanitri.

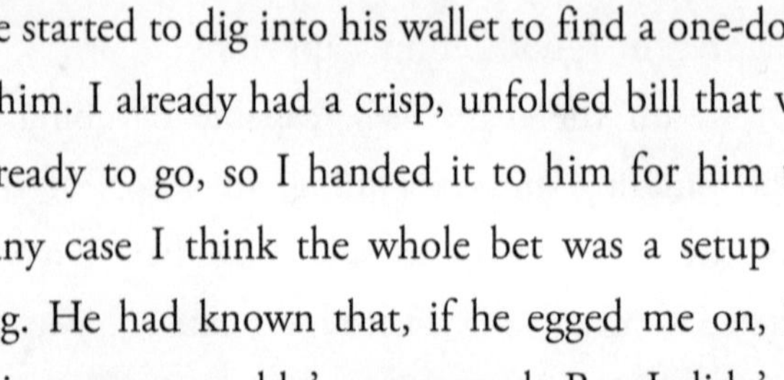

Communicating expectations is a critical thing to do. But it is a two-way street. You must communicate what you want your team to do to be successful. When they go home at the end of the day, they need to be able to know if they had a good day. But, on the flip side, as a leader you also have to allow your team to document their expectations of you, in terms of what they need to get their jobs done. And you need to keep showing up every day to give your team updates on your commitments to them. The plan will succeed if you do these two things. It will fail if you don't.

CHAPTER 6

Letting the Plan Fail

With you folks behind me, I'm not worried about where Delta's going...Just run Delta along the lines we've established and twenty to thirty years from now, it will be the most outstanding transportation system in America.
–C.E. Woolman

At best, I'm a slightly sub-.500 coach. On average, during the regular season, my teams win just under half of all the games we play, every season. It's not that I do that on purpose. I'd love to go out there and win them all. But I've learned that sometimes you have to lose in order to win big in the end.

One of my favorite things in the world is coaching youth baseball and softball. To me, there aren't too many things that beat watching children take a game that they love and use it to channel their energy and emotion into raw excitement and exhilaration. I especially love watching that kid who's been struggling all year at the plate get to the last game and hit a walk-off single as their teammates mob them at first base—or when they catch a pop-fly in the outfield to end the game after starting the season being too afraid of the ball to catch a toss from their mom or dad.

However, the best sound, to me, isn't the one the kid makes as they pump their fist into the air, hooting and hollering as they relish in being the unlikely hero. I wait and listen for the dad or mom jumping up and down, so proud of their kid, bursting at the seams as they wait to congratulate their son or daughter as they come off the field. They waited all season for that moment, and I finally was able to find a way to work with their kid to get there. I've been that dad, and it is the best thing in the world seeing your kid do the improbable.

Let me be frank, though. I do love winning. And I do get a bit depressed every time one of my teams loses. Just ask Catherine how losing and winning affects my mood on Saturday evenings. It doesn't matter if it's 8U coach-pitch baseball or a highly competitive travel softball tournament. As a coach, it hurts to lose. And it feels so damned good to win. But there are times when I *really* want to win, and I'm willing to sacrifice the times when it doesn't matter as much in order to make those important wins happen.

As a recreational league coach, you have to realize that every team makes the playoffs when you get to the end of the season. It's not like they tell you that you can't play in the end-of-season tournament because you went 0-15. We're not in the pros, here. There're eight-year-olds out there. Everyone makes the dang tournament. That's how the league makes their money! And if you are going to win the tournament, guess what? You're eventually going to have to beat the best teams in the league. So, what difference does it really make whether you finish the regular season in first place or in last place? Tournament seeding isn't *that* important in eight-, nine-, and ten-year-olds' sports!

I've never had any of my teams finish the regular season in first place. We're usually right in the middle of the pack. But we've won the tournament a couple of time and placed second a whole bunch of times. In the end, we are always able to compete with the best teams on the last day—and, in the end, I think that's all I really want for my players. Nobody wants to get slaughtered. If you're going to lose, you want it to be competitive. You want to have the best teams out there respect your ability to play. And you want to be able to sit your team down at the end of the last game and have them be proud of how they played. Even if they have to wipe away a few tears along the way when they lose.

A couple of years ago, when my daughter, Evelyn, was really starting to get into softball, I agreed to take on her team as the head coach. I hadn't really done that before. I didn't really understand very much about coaching girls, quite frankly. I'd had about seven seasons coaching my son's baseball teams, so I understood boys—plus it helped that I was one.

A few things stuck with me for a long time from watching the different approaches that various coaches took in that first season. It was an 8U age group, which meant all of the girls were either seven or eight years old on January 1st of that year. We started out with arguably the worst draft picks in the league. In fact, at the end of the first week of practice, I stayed late with a couple of the other dad coaches, and they asked me if I had forgotten to draft players in the first two rounds. We looked that bad. I was a little worried that our girls weren't going to have a lot of fun since we dads were all fairly convinced we were going to lose every game—by a lot.

Resigned to the idea, all of my assistant coaches and I agreed that four out of the eleven girls on our team were probably more interested in building sandcastles in the dirt than learning how to be fielders. We'd teach them the basics, but it was obviously not worth spending a ton of time trying to teach them to be middle infielders. We sent them to the batting cages a whole lot. If anything, we'd at least get them all to hit! We'd need the runs. And they'd have more fun hitting than daydreaming in the field, anyway.

Of the seven fielders we had that showed some actual potential for developing fielding skills, four of them could consistently catch a ball. Getting actual outs in the field (meaning anything that isn't a strikeout) is hard at this age. A lot of things have to go right. The ball has to be hit pretty much right at a player, to start out. Then that fielder must cleanly field the ball, which is about a 50-50 proposition, at best, even with our most talented players. Then they need to throw this giant ball that's three times bigger than their hand across the field to a girl standing on first base, 30 feet away, on target. And miraculously, the player on first base must catch that oversized ball in their awkward glove that looks like it was either sized for Barbie or Andre the Giant. It seems they only make two sizes. Neither size is appropriate for an eight-year-old girl.

Our first game was a high-scoring affair. We had exactly one out in the field. The rest of our defensive strategy involved putting hexes on the opposing team's coach, hoping that they would inadvertently strike out their own players. This was a coach-pitch league, so the offensive strategy is to find the coach on your team who does the best job of hitting each girl's bat with the ball. If the other team's coach isn't very good at this, you have a chance at winning games.

During this high-scoring affair, we overthrew first base a staggering number of times (probably at least ten). We kept trying, though. The one out we did get was our pitcher catching a fly ball to end the game. We won the game 13-12. Thank goodness the other team had a bunch of sandcastle builders on their squad too. They played even less defense than we did. They didn't get any outs in the field.

The overthrows to first base were actually the winning key to our strategy that season. I didn't even recognize it as a strategy until much later in the season. In fact, if I had thought of doing what the other teams started to do, I probably would have rethought our whole defensive scheme. You see, we coaches were too stupid to tell our girls to stop throwing to first base. They kept throwing the ball away, over, around, under the legs of, or through our first baseman so often I lost count. The other teams we played against adopted a different way of getting outs. They instructed their pitchers to get the ball and just run down the batter-runners and try to outsprint the base runners to each force-out base. They had their other players just hold the ball when they got it and run it to the pitcher's rubber, which is what stops runners from running.

This strategy was at least 40-50% effective, as long as you put your speediest players in at the pitcher position. And 40-50% is way better than the 0% that we were achieving. Early on in the season, especially when we started to play the teams that had actually drafted well, we took some lumps in the loss column. The other coaches, with their strategy of running my base runners down with their pitcher, were winning against my "throw every ball past first base" strategy.

But then something happened that stated to turn the tide. One of my first basemen, Caroline[20], started catching almost every ball that came close to her. Apparently, she had gotten so upset after the first couple of games when she missed some of the throws that she worked really hard and practiced at home a bunch with her dad. And before mid-season, things were finally coming together for her. Suddenly my "throw every ball past first base" strategy had to get revised to a "throw two-thirds of everything past first base" strategy. After all, I could only play Caroline at that position for one third of the game due to park rules. We had a rule that a player could only play a position for two innings per game. This forced coaches to try out girls in lots of positions during the games.

But then another funny thing started to happen. Carter, one of my other players who was starting to develop into a

20 Caroline is now an amazing first baseman and is constantly a number one draft pick in our league. It helps that she can hit the ball to the fence regularly. It also helps when you can do the splits and catch a ball at the same time, as a first baseman. Tampa Bay's Ji-Man Choi would be impressed.

competitive player, started to see Caroline catch balls at first base, and that gave her more confidence to do the same thing. So, she became a lot less afraid of this big, yellow ball coming at her and started to be another reliable baseman for me. Then her friend, Aidan, didn't want to be left out, and by game number five, we got a whole four outs in the field! That may still sound pretty pathetic, but when you start with one out in the field in your first game, you'll take a 300% improvement, any day.

Every game kept getting better throughout the rest of the season. The other coaches were still deathly afraid of having their girls throwing anything to anyone, so if the play was out of reach for the girl to run down the play herself, they instituted a strategy of "hold the ball." That way, you kept the ball from getting thrown to the fence-line like we had done in the first few games, and you kept your eye out for opportunities for rundowns.

By the time we got to the end-of-season tournament, it was clear whose strategy had been the better of the two. Our team—thanks to the constant focus of getting the bottom of our talent pool to focus on hitting all the time in practice—started putting up offensive numbers that were really impressive. Even my worst hitter was hitting .333 by the end of the season (and yes, I keep stats on 8U girls' softball—don't judge me). And the defenses we were playing against were only nominally better than they had been at the beginning of the season since nobody had bothered to actually develop any kind of a throwing game. So, we were putting up 12, 13, and 15 runs per game against these "run-and-hold" defenses.

Meanwhile, our defense was getting stiflingly good compared to the competition. Keep in mind, stifling at this age means you get at least half of your outs in the field. We were getting long outs from third base to first base once or twice per game. That's not a distance that you can get someone out by running across the infield diamond. We were the only team in the league making those throws and catches.

We ended up cakewalking through the championship. Our closest game was 4-0 in the tournament: we just weren't hitting well that day. We also had two very untimely double plays we ran into that both ended bases-loaded rallies. The next morning, we pasted the 1st place team 15-1 in the semi-finals before dispatching the 2nd place team 16-7 for the championship title. I have a big trophy in my bedroom commemorating that tournament reminding me every day of the importance of letting people fail a little bit in order to win.

In business, if you want to succeed in the long term, you have got to learn to allow your people to fail. And you absolutely cannot let it be a big deal. Failing is just a part of the process of learning. Your job is to make sure that you never put people in a position where, when they do fail, they will lose you more money than you can afford, get themselves (or others) hurt, or die (or cause others to die). As long as you safeguard against those three things, your business will be just fine.

Just like my softball opponents, if you never learn that it's critical to let people fail, you end up never actually developing a team that can do things on their own without you. You have to walk away and let your people start to figure things out for themselves. In fact, here's the best thing you can possibly do—once you have laid out your plan and effectively communicated expectations: don't do a thing. Sit back, watch what your people do, and wait to see how well they do with the execution.

You are a coach. This is not a metaphor. You are literally a coach. Just like a softball team, the coach isn't supposed to play the game. As much as I would have loved to suit up and play the game myself, they would have checked my birth certificate and thrown me out of the park. A good coach lets the players play the game after fully teaching them the rules and practicing enough with them to make sure they can apply the rules. Teaching them the rules and practicing is comparable to holding meetings where you introduce a plan and confirm that all the stakeholders have bought into the plan, then setting up metrics for them to be able to gauge their own progress.

Now it's time for your team to play. So, stop jawing at them. It's game time. Game time is not the time for instruction. It's the time for succeeding or failing. Did you ever see Bill Belichick go out and try to teach Tom Brady how to read a nickel defense during a football game against the Buffalo Bills? Or Bobby Cox going out to the mound to try to teach Greg Maddux how to throw a slider while Barry Bonds is standing there in the batter's box? Then why in the world would you think it's okay to micromanage your project manager every day to make sure she's doing her job right? The time to teach is *before* or maybe *between* games, not in the *middle* of one.

Look, you're going to find either one of two things. Either you've hired well, or you haven't. If you have—and if you've got a good plan and you've set your expectations clearly—then, even though there will be mistakes made along the way, you're going to win more times than you're going to lose. If you haven't hired well, you're going to notice that you're losing more times than you're winning, so you need to make a change. Either you'll need to *change* the people you have—or you'll need to change the *people* you have.

By the end of every softball season, my goal is to be able to shut up and watch the game. If my girls on the field can learn to not need me and act as a team without me doing anything except fill out a line-up card, occasionally make a trip to the pitcher's mound, and coordinate snacks and drinks for after the game, then it's been a success. It's the same strategy in business. Your goal needs to be to get to the point, as quickly as you can, where your business no longer needs you to be there, other than to make sure you've got the right people, make the occasional coaching moment happen when things go wrong, and reward the team with some snacks and (adult) drinks.

The most mature thing you can ever do, as a leader, is to not get consumed by the fear of failure. It's okay if people fail, as long as they are learning from their mistakes and the mistakes are small. It's even desirable, as long as the failure doesn't cost more money than you can afford to lose or result in an unsafe situation. Put your people in a position to occasionally fail so that they learn, and you'll have a pipeline of future leaders growing within your own group. Fail to do this and the team will never grow beyond your own ability to micromanage. And

I'll tell you right now, you're not as good as you think you are at micromanaging people.

Oh, and your people hate it, too. They told me so.

The number one reason that good people make the decision to leave a position is that they don't feel that they are given the opportunity to fail. Don't believe me? Look at the number of Blue Chip NCAA athletes that transfer schools every year because they are simply not getting the playing time they think they can get at another school. They'll often forego an entire year of eligibility to get a chance to be a starter at another school. And it's all about their coach not being ready to trust them because they're convinced that they'll go out and screw up. And, yeah, that coach might be right: the rookie isn't going to be perfect right out of the box.

Last year, the University of Georgia lost one of the most highly recruited, five-star quarterbacks they had on their roster to Ohio State because the freshman QB didn't think he was going to be trusted with the starting QB job soon enough. His coach at Georgia wasn't willing to fail for a few games while he learned the ropes. He was more afraid of fans being upset at losing a game or two than developing the future. Ohio State ended up with a great QB, and it led them to a Final Four finish, ahead of the Georgia Bulldogs in 2019. As a Georgia Tech guy, I was not heartbroken about this.

Of course, sometimes people have unrealistic expectations of what they should be trusted to do. You need to use good judgment with this. But you do need to challenge yourself with this question: am I constantly trying to work myself out of a job by letting those around me start to learn how to take over my role? As much as it might sound bad to do this, it should be the absolute goal of every true leader—to work yourself out of a job. Every true leader, at their core, should want themselves to be irrelevant in their current position within three years or less so that the company can use them to expand in other areas and either build onto their team or build brand new teams. It's the strategy that gets you freed up to look to the next challenge.

If you have not already done so, create a plan to become irrelevant. Communicate this plan to your teammates, who will need to take over each of the things that you are responsible for doing right now. Work with them over a period of time to transfer these responsibilities. Train them, monitor their ability to do the work, and then be there to catch them when they fall down here or there. You're not going to purposefully set them up for a failure and watch them ride off a cliff, but you do need to let them give things a try for themselves, knowing they will learn from their missteps.

One day, you'll find they don't need training wheels anymore, at which point you can, and should, step away. But you've got to let them have their failure first. It's the only way to learn so they can understand for themselves how to make the plan better over time. In the next chapter we'll talk about how to sit down and talk about the failures that do occur. But for now, we have to prepare ourselves for the inevitability of failure and the need for it to occur.

C.E. Woolman understood this concept. In the opening quote to this chapter, he clearly gets the idea of establishing a legacy. He was nearing the sunset of his career at 68 years old[21], clearly happy with the team he had built around him, and he felt confident that he could step away and let his team do their job and that they'd know what to do. He surely anticipated that they'd make mistakes, but he knew that they were ready to take the helm for the next 20 to 30 years into the future. Every company needs to be that forward-looking and to be able to get their leadership team to the point where that level of trust is built. That message resonated with the Delta team for decades to come. Our leaders trusted us to do our jobs. The CEO's that guided us out of our most recent challenges were from a long line of Delta leaders who believed in this way of working, and we had these timeless reminders from our founder that we needed to build teams in a way that allowed us to pass on the torch.

That's what leadership demands.

Of all the leaders I got to work with across Delta, my all-time favorite is a guy called Jerry Allen. Jerry was the vice president of Line Maintenance when I was at Delta[22]. This is the group of thousands of mechanics at Delta Tech Ops that

---

21 In 1957, Woolman had served as the leader of Delta Air Lines for 12 years. He would serve another nine years at Delta, until his death on September 11, 1966. His later years were spent building Delta's legacy as a major player in the new jet age of commercial aviation.

22 Since I departed, Jerry took over almost the entire front-line operations team, which consists of roughly 75 percent of all personnel within Tech Ops - a division that, overall, has had 10,000-plus employees.

carry out maintenance on the whole fleet all over the world, whether it is freezing in Detroit in the middle of January or if it's 110 degrees on the ramp in Phoenix in August. These guys are battle-hardened warriors who have to keep these aircraft airworthy in some of the most hellish conditions on the planet, and they have to be accurate, work with precision, and solve problems in less-than-ideal environments: in addition, they've usually got a lot of angry people waiting for them to finish up, like the people staring at them from the gate area, when the flight is already an hour past schedule.

To understand Jerry, here's a few things you need to know. His home base is in Salt Lake City, Utah, where he raised his family and served time in his church as a bishop for several years. The plan he follows is God's plan, and he doesn't care who you are—he'll tell you your plan for him gets trumped by that one every time. He is dedicated to his community in Salt Lake, but he works in Atlanta. Every week, he flies into Atlanta and drives a cheap 1990s four-door sedan for which he couldn't have paid more than a couple of thousand dollars. He bought it used. Although he's only the second owner, it's the same car that each of his three teenage kids drove when they were in high school. He could easily afford to drive a Ferrari, if he really wanted to, but that would be too flashy for him. He stays in a modest crash pad with no frills, even though he could afford to live in a lavish executive suite in mid-town.

If you search for anything about him on Google, you'll find exactly nothing useful. You'll get no pictures of him. He doesn't do Facebook, and the one or two sites that have anything at all on them with his name will probably not be there in six months. Jerry doesn't tolerate nonsense. He doesn't drink, and he never uses profanity. But if you piss him off, he'll give you a look that seems to convey every horrifying swear word you ever learned on the playground in the fourth grade.

Jerry's career at Delta has been focused around Line Maintenance. He's a mechanic's mechanic. Very practical. He always thinks of his workers first. He's the true embodiment of a servant leader. His workers respect him because he holds everyone accountable for what they are supposed to provide to the ultimate end-user in the maintenance world—the guy way out on an island working on an airplane with the most basic tools and equipment, trying to get a job done with nothing but a computer, a telephone, a bag of tools, and (maybe) a truck.

Now, at Tech Ops, the line mechanic is somewhat of an unsung hero. He can move Heaven and Earth to find a way to get that airplane fixed, saving the day for a couple of hundred passengers who never knew he existed, or he can do the same thing under virtually the same conditions and every one of those passengers can be cursing him for not being fast enough. Nobody ever looks at the line mechanic and says, "Hey, that guy did a really good job. Thanks to him, our flight left on time." It's more likely that the same passenger, under slightly different circumstances says, "Geez, why is it taking that guy so long to put duct tape on that cracked piece of plastic?"

Before Jerry was entrusted with the entire Line Maintenance operation, Delta had steadily been improving operations, year after year. We already talked about how the Line Maintenance organization started to use KPIs to drive down maintenance cancellations to unprecedented industry levels. His predecessor,

Lee, had done some really good things, but Jerry wanted to take things to a new level during his tenure by setting a new expectation with his team. One of the most critical things he implemented was a truly simple concept: stop trying to be the hero that hides a bad plan.

The problem with heroes, in a corporate environment, is that if you keep doing hero work every day, you never improve the support systems that are supposed to put you in a position where you *don't have* to be a hero in order to succeed. Sometimes, as painful as it sounds, you have to just work the plan. And if the plan sucks, then guess what? All you're doing is disguising that fact by forcing it to work all the time. Even though it's a bad plan, no one ever sees that the plan was bad to begin with because the hero makes it hard to see that there is actually a problem. Besides, eventually the heroism gets old and tiring, and the person doing the extra work gets burned out and stops.

It's a zero-sum game. Jerry understood this.

What was happening, too often, was that our planned maintenance would involve work that was impossible to accomplish as laid out in the plan. Perhaps the material that was needed wasn't available, the work required tools that they didn't have, the downtime the aircraft was given wasn't long enough to do the task that was on the job card, or maybe it was one of a litany of other issues that prevented the mechanic out on the line from being successful. The crews and their leaders felt like it was their job to figure out a way to make those tasks work, even though they weren't planned well. The result was that they'd pull an extra crew member or two off another task to help get the one done that required more time to do than the time allotted. Or they'd have to call Engineering to get a material substitution for a part they didn't have available. These things stressed the system, ate up time, and caused downstream deferrals of the tasks that they otherwise would have been able to handle.

Jerry recognized something simple but extremely important. If we were going to continue to set records with our reliability, we simply had to become the best planners on the planet. And, if we never worked to the plan and had to try to shoehorn everything into a box that had been built too small, then we'd never be the world's best planning organization. His task was to get his leaders to set the expectation that the crews out in the field needed to spend most of their time focusing—not on the non-routine, fire-fighting that had to happen to make bad plans work, day in and day out—but on the routine, well-planned tasks that keep the overall fleet health high. In other words, they needed to focus their attention on the work that is actually well planned every day and prioritize that work over the emergencies caused by not having a good setup.

This is a classic case of not letting 20% of your problems consume 80% of your time. With a Line Maintenance organization, time is your most precious resource. What you choose to spend your time on is the most important decision you make each day. If you are spending the majority of your time on the distractions that bad planning creates, and you have to work harder on those issues—because it's typically harder to fix issues where you don't have the right parts, or the engineering is wrong, or some other issue crops up that forces you to slow down—then that's where you really start to burn up your time. The sacrifice is that you didn't get the 80% done, which is the work that would have been much easier to take care of.

The hard part, for Jerry's leaders, was setting the expectation that it was okay to let the plan fail—that, in fact, it is absolutely the *right* thing to do. Nobody wants to have to come into the office in the morning and explain why their crews left a bunch of unscheduled AOS aircraft unfinished. That looks bad on their team. We're all trained from the beginning of our career that you do whatever it takes to *not* have your team look bad. But, sometimes looking good today covers up fundamental problems, and that fear of looking bad can cause your goal to fail tomorrow and the next day. The big, overarching goal is to figure out how to avoid a maintenance cancellation at a reasonable cost. It was counterintuitive to allow this goal to be compromised in the interest of fixing systemic problems with tasks that would become repeat issues every week.

After some consternation and heated debate with his team, Jerry sat his directors down and gave them all an order to take each of their stations across the network and make two teams at each airport. The first team would consist of the majority of the mechanics available, and they would do nothing but work the exact maintenance tasks allocated by the planning team with everything that was needed to complete the tasks. The second team would be a much smaller, highly skilled team that would focus their efforts on emergencies and unplanned work that he considered to be disruptive. If the emergency and unplanned work was more than that small crew could fix, then so be it. He told his leaders that he would personally take the blame anytime those results got scrutinized by senior leadership. That ended the conversation.

This is why I really like Jerry. He will wear you out when he knows he's right. And he'll also take the blame when he tells you to do something, and bad things happen. He's smart enough to know that you have to let things fail if you want them to get better. When they fail, he's learned that it's important to track the reasons *why* they failed. He understands that the concept of striving for zero defects means that you have to be relentless in finding the reasons why things fail. But if you never let failures happen, you never expose the real problems. And if you never expose the problems in your operation, *they* will expose *you*. And then it really *is* your fault that it happened. You enabled it!

This is the other, more important reason why I like Jerry. He doesn't care what anyone thinks about him. You could fire him tomorrow, and he'd just shrug and head back to Salt Lake City. In his head, he'd maybe think about calling you some really nasty curse word, but out of his mouth all you might hear is something about you being a jack wagon—that's about as bad a word as will come out of his mouth. He's figured out that he's good enough at doing what he does that his boss trusts him, even if bad things happen here and there. And he's also figured out that the day his boss isn't smart enough to trust him is probably the day he should go ahead and retire.

Failing so you can succeed comes out of the mindset that we need to keep improving on what others might assume has been perfected. Most of the airline industry would have looked at what we had already achieved with our cancellation rates and considered it unimprovable. We already talked about the fact that Delta has been constantly beating its own records when it comes to cancel-free days, year after year. What do you do when you get to over 200 of these days each year? Do you spike the football, claim victory, and find something else to focus on? Most companies would. Jerry didn't. He started to let the plan fail a little and then watched his team grow cancel-free days to over 300 each year. What do you do after that? You keep shining a spotlight on every failure until the people who caused them eliminates the reason for them permanently.

In 2010, alone, Tech Ops was responsible for cancelling over 5,600 flights. In 2018, thanks to the building blocks that had been put in place with important and relevant KPIs and the leadership of Jerry, Tech Ops was only responsible for 55 cancellations. That's over 100 times better! In 2019, he drove the team to reach 100 consecutive days with no maintenance cancellations. That's about as close as you can get to perfection, folks. But I'm sure Jerry's out there, right now, getting his guys to zero in on 365. And I will not be very surprised when I see them do it.

CHAPTER 7

Picking Up the Pieces

I'm optimistic about the future of air transportation. The introduction of the jets has created a lot of problems. But this industry grew up on problems—and it grew because it solved them.
–C.E. Woolman

On September 14, 2005, Delta Air Lines, Inc., filed for Chapter 11 bankruptcy protection. It was my fault. I didn't do enough to prevent it from happening. In fact, it was the fault of all of us collectively. It wasn't the previous CEO's fault. It wasn't the terrorists from 9/11 that made our business plan fail (although they didn't help), and we couldn't blame the geopolitical issues that had caused rising fuel costs for us having lost all of our money. It was *our* fault.

We hired a consultant to tell us this. We paid them a lot of money to bring us all into a room and point a finger right at us and tell us that *we* were the reason that our company just went belly up. And do you know what? It was some of the best money we ever spent. We needed someone to come in and slap us hard across the face with that fact. When going into Chapter 11, we all felt nice and sorry for ourselves. It was always someone or something else that was the reason we were in such a bad position. Woe is us. Poor airlines just can't catch a break. We had all sorts of reasons why we were losing money: the war, the recession, bad leadership. The list went on and on. But none of us put *ourselves* on that list of reasons. None of us thought that *we* were complicit in the historic, grim reality that we had been a part of a dying, major air carrier.

For too many years, we had taken pride in being the best example of the worst business model in the airline industry. I kept a political cartoon pinned up in my cubicle for years that showed little cartoon airplanes desperately flapping their wings in front of a huge airplane engine that was ready to chop them up into little pieces. The big cartoon engine had the word "bankruptcy" on it. That cartoon epitomized how we at Delta felt about ourselves. The first little airplane that was about to get digested by the engine was US Airways. Next up was American Airlines. Then United, and out in front were Continental, Northwest, and Delta. Our thought was, "Hey, we're doing really bad, but at least we're not US Airways!"

As a business, that's a really horrible way to think. And it quickly leads to complacency. When you are constantly comparing yourself to other really bad, failing businesses, you've got your heads, collectively, up your behinds. But that's where we were back then. We literally had to hire someone to come in and kick us hard in the butt to start thinking differently. To teach us, they played a lot of games with us to show us how we were thinking—and then to teach us how to think differently. At the time, my pay grade wasn't high enough to warrant an invitation to this training, but it made such an impact on the Delta leadership, it became Delta lore and I still remember a lot of the lessons that came out of that engagement.

One of the games they played is an older game that was popularized in the 1970s, which is why it worked on our team. It had run its course by the early 2000s so none of the participants were familiar with it. The consultants gave everyone some really simple rules. They divided the room of employees into six groups, and they gave each group two chips. One was red, and the other one was blue.

Each team was told that the object of the game was to score the most points possible. And here's how the game worked. Each team would get all of their players together, and they would strategize over which of the two chips to play in each round. There would be five rounds of play. If one team played the blue chip and the other team played a red chip, the team that played the red chip would get two points, and the team that played the blue chip would get zero points. If both teams played the red chip, both teams would only get one point. But if both teams played the blue chip, both teams would score five points. In each round, every team would go head-to-head with each of the other teams. Each team had to make sure their choice was unanimous before playing each chip.

It was a simple game. The consultants explained the rules and then went to sit down and observe and said nothing. They watched as the game got going. And then things started to get competitive. It all started out as you might think. Some teams started by playing nice by playing the blue chips. But most of the other teams quickly capitalized on this by playing red chips to try to outmaneuver the other teams and get ahead of them. Mid-round, almost every team that had started out with the blue chips were getting annihilated, so they gave up and just played the red ones from then on out. By the end of the game, everyone was playing red, and nobody was getting any advantage over the other.

In each class, the result always came to the same type of end, just as described. The exact scores would vary, but at the end of each game of five rounds, there would always be one team that had scored more points that all of the others, and they would hoot and holler and perform little victory celebrations, rubbing all of the other teams' noses in their losses.

And then, like clockwork, the consultant would come over and break down the results. Invariably, the winning team would have somewhere between 35 and 40 points. The losing team might only have 20 to 25 points. Then the consultant asked the entire class, "So, who won?" And, depending on who got the most points, the class would point to that team and declare them the winners.

The consultant would look at the team who got the most points and ask them, "So, remind me, how many points did your team get?" They'd give the answer she already knew, and then she would ask, "And how many points was it possible to get in this game?" With some quick math, they'd reply, "One hundred twenty-five." And then you started to see everyone start to get it, as the consultant pointed out, "So you got 40 points out of 125 and you call yourselves winners?" This is when you'd typically have one guy in the back of the room say, "Well, we got more points than everyone else!"

The game always works the same way—it is so predictable. The object of the game, as stated in the beginning, wasn't to get more points than everyone else. The object of the game was to "score the most points possible." Nobody won! In fact, nobody got to even a third of the points required to "win." In almost every team, someone immediately jumps up and says, "I knew it—I told you guys! Nobody listened!" Then the consultants would overhear that comment, stop everything, and remind everyone of the only rule in the game, which was that all decisions needed to be unanimous. If there was one person on a team who strongly thought that everyone was doing the wrong thing, then why hadn't they stopped everyone from making bad decisions?

This was why it was the fault of all of us. This wasn't really a game; this was a re-enactment! This was the way all of us thought in the airline industry. And it was just wrong. We all assumed, like most businesses, that the best way to make sure we survived was if another business competing in the same industry was doing worse than we were. None of us stopped to even think about the idea that winning didn't necessarily mean that everyone else has to lose. Even if someone did think it, nobody stood up and did anything about it.

There were six teams in this game. Was it a coincidence that six major airlines were teetering on the edge of bankruptcy or were already in bankruptcy at that time? We were all so busy trying to compare ourselves with the other five that we lost track of what we were trying to do—make the most money possible. We were playing the game wrong. We learned, as a company, by playing a stupid, simple game, that we had a fundamental flaw in our way of thinking.

Over the next decade, we did things a lot better. Of the six major airlines that existed in the mid-2000s, three are still left today—United, American, and Delta. And really, United is actually Continental. American is actually US Airways (which was actually America West). And we are a 50-50 blend between Delta and Northwest. But the surviving three brands had a wildly successful decade. It didn't take one of us losing money for the rest of us to make money. In fact, the past decade has been a golden age of commercial aviation. No other period in time has been more profitable, year in and year out. And nobody "lost." In fact, everybody who played the game "won."

I think we got the point of the game. But would we have if someone hadn't come over and smacked us upside the head to show us? In a way, we had to get someone to do something drastic to change our mindset and get us to stop feeling sorry for ourselves and to start doing things that would make us profitable. We had to have someone who wasn't afraid to hurt our feelings by holding a mirror in front of our faces and telling us to look at all of the dumb things we were doing. And, if not for this, I'd argue that we'd never have looked hard enough at changing and getting better.

As we saw in the last chapter, it's hard for any leader to let people around them fail. The only harder thing to do is to pull aside the team member who failed and *tell* them about their failure. The reason this is so hard is that most of the time, the guy who failed doesn't know he failed. And none of us really wants to be the one who has to tell him. That's why consultants make so much money, folks. It's much easier to pay an independent third party to come into your company and tell your people that they suck than to tell them yourself!

Save yourself some money and learn the art of picking up the pieces yourself. If you do things right, your people are going to fail a lot. But if you want to capitalize on that failure and let the learning process do wonderful things, you have to learn how to pull people aside and tell them they're terrible, while also figuring out how to do it so they don't get demoralized. After all, you wanted them to have a chance to fail, right? You did kind of plan on that happening. Were you expecting them to realize their mistakes on their own every time they screwed up?

As their leader, you have the fun job of letting people know that they aren't perfect. And, most of the time, you have to do this in real time as mistakes get made. It doesn't need to be the exact moment or day when they made the mistake, but it's got to be done in a timely fashion. Otherwise, the mistake may be repeated so many times that you can't dig yourself out of the hole you've fallen into. You also need to make sure that it's just you and that person, one-on-one, when you tell them this. Never tell someone that they screwed up in front of someone else. In fact, it's really important that nobody around you even *knows* that you are about to have a conversation about that person's failure.

With the two of you behind a closed door, you've set up the moment to be all about positive coaching instead of a public flogging. This is important because you're usually not mad at the person who made an error because that's what it was—an unintentional *error*. You liked this person well enough to trust them with some part of your business. Just because they made an error does not mean you stop liking and respecting them. Similarly, you entrusted them with a part of your plan, so you expected, at some point, to have to talk about them not executing the plan. No big deal.

Now, every case is different, so I'm not going to be able to tell you what you need to say to that person, but I will tell you that you need to avoid putting them on the defensive. There's nothing to be gained from making someone feel like they need to put up a wall so they don't get hurt. Focus on the facts. Remind that person about agreements that you've made with each other. Review what you put in the plan. Then simply go through what you saw happen and ask them tough questions about how they feel things went.

I believe in the Socratic method, the idea that people learn best when they aren't told the answer directly and that the learning moment comes when you ask the question that leads them to realize the lesson on their own, without you spoon-feeding it to them. I recommend this method when you're giving people feedback on their recent failure. You don't want to start with all guns blazing, ripping into them, and tearing them down. You want them to have that "Aha!" moment where they figure out for themselves what they did. The chances are much higher that they'll embrace the next steps if they figure out for themselves what happened, rather than you tell them.

The game with the red and blue chips was all about self-realization. The reason I still remember people talking about it is because it wasn't an idea that was shoved down anyone's throats during a lecture.

But that's the beauty of what they did there. Almost 15 years later, I can tell you more about what that consultant did in that week-long class than I can tell you about what I ate for breakfast last Monday. Hell, I could probably completely reconstruct the entire week-long course. Why? Because people came back to the office and talked about it so much. There were many "Aha!" moments that had been so meaningful to the people who took the course that they told everyone else what they learned and about all the ways we were screwing up as a company.

The art of having people recognize their mistakes on their own is, first and foremost, an art. We talked earlier about style. This is another situation in which style is important, because you have to develop your own style of telling people about their failures. Your style will be different for small errors versus big errors, and it will be different from first-time offenses versus repeat offenses. And when it is an intentional disregard instead of unintentional error—boy oh boy, you'd better have a style prepared for that, too!

Just as I occasionally have to do with my kids, there are times where it is appropriate to express disappointment in a dramatic way. There are times where raising your voice is completely appropriate. It's rare. But there are times. However, most of the time, your tone is going to be purely positive. After all, you are their coach, not their parent. If they act like kids, then yes, react the way you would with a kid—but save this for when it is warranted. It's usually not.

In the fall of 2014, I remember sitting in one of Jerry Allen's early afternoon operations teleconference calls. Three times a day, every day of the week, all of the support teams gathered in Atlanta into a conference room and sat around a horseshoe-shaped table. The meeting leader (which was usually Jerry or one of his directors or general managers) opened up a conference line to the Maintenance Control Center (the MCC), which is located across the runway from the Tech Ops hangar, and all of the station managers called in from all over the world. We talked about every aircraft that was currently AOS, and we went over the game plan for getting them all back into service.

A week earlier, a violent windstorm at JFK had caused a ladder on the tarmac to be lifted up and slammed into the lower skin panel of the horizontal stabilizer on one of our Boeing 737-800 jets. Fixing this panel involved a couple of days of labor removing the panel, a few days fixing it, and then a couple more days reinstalling it back on the stabilizer structure. This was a pretty big task, and it was made a lot more difficult by the fact that the job had to be done in an awkward area high up off the ground.

The JFK team had spent the past week doing all the tasks to remove, repair, and install the damaged panel back on the wing. The day that they got ready to do the installation, an inspector noticed that the stabilizer spar structure was dented, and so they would need to get an engineering evaluation prior to having the panel reinstalled. I was the engineering manager who was responsible for providing that review, so on this particular day, I leaned into the microphone to give my report on the status of our review.

I had had pictures of the dent printed out and had brought them with me to show the other leaders so they could understand what I was referring to when I told them that it was going to take some extra time to review. I mentioned, at the end of my update, that it would have been a lot more helpful to have noticed this dent on day three instead of day seven. That way, we would have had the time to evaluate it without causing the whole aircraft to be out of service a couple more days while we did our structural review. I pointed at the picture, which showed this huge, obvious dent right there in the spar. I said something to the effect of, "I can't see how you could miss a huge dent like that for *four* days."

Joe Santos, one of Jerry's leaders, was running the call that day. I passed out a few copies of the pictures in both directions around the table so everyone could see the damage. A few of the other leaders in the room shook their heads, looked back up at me, and shrugged in agreement with my comments. With that little update out of the way, the team went on to the several other aircraft on the AOS list. Boston Line Maintenance checked in. LAX checked in. Narita, Detroit, Atlanta, and Salt Lake all reviewed their issues, and I chimed in on a couple of actions my team was taking, as was appropriate. It was a typical day in the life of the 13:00 ops call.

The next day, I was sitting in my office with the usual line of people outside my door coming in and out with various issues of the day. Joe Santos came in and asked if he could sit down for a minute. I said, "Sure, Joe! What can I do to help?" Joe is a native of Boston. The JFK Line Maintenance team reported to him. Occasionally, he came down to Atlanta for the week to take care of business with his boss, Jerry. While in Atlanta, he would do things like run Jerry's ops meetings, follow up on issues brought up on the calls, have his regular one-on-one meeting with his boss, and take care of any business he had in our headquarters city. He was on one of these trips that week.

Joe was very calm when he visited me. He asked me how I was doing. He asked how my family was doing. Then he told me, "You know, I wanted to talk with you yesterday, but I was too angry to come in here, so I waited until I cooled down a bit."

I was trying to remember what day it had been the day before. Was it taco day yesterday? Then I remembered. Yes, it had been taco day. Then I tried to think about what else happened. But nothing popped out at me, so I just gave Joe a dumb look.

He helped to jog my memory a bit. He said, "You know, you probably didn't realize it, but what you said on the 13:00 call really pissed off my guys in JFK."

Now I started to remember. Windstorm. Ladder damage. The dent. 737-800. JFK.

Yeah...but I still gave him that same stupid look. Why would his guys have been upset at what I said?

Joe pulled up his phone and held it up for me and explained. "While you were passing around that picture of the dent on that stabilizer and pointing out to everyone in the room how obvious the dent was and that we should have caught it four days earlier, my phone started lighting up with text messages from my guys in JFK."

Oh. Right. Now I was starting to anticipate the next thing he was going to say. So, I offered up my guess. I said, "I kind of threw them under the bus on that, didn't I?"

Joe quietly nodded his head and then added, "My station manager wanted to know who you were so he could come down to Atlanta and strangle you," he added, "You know, it's really easy to see that dent when you zoom in on a 10-times magnified view like you had with that picture you were passing around."

Again, I saw where he was going with that. Try finding that same dent in the rain from the ground, staring up at a spar that's 20 feet away, right? I mentioned something to that effect. Joe nodded his head.

Joe saw that I understood what I had done. He also saw that I hadn't done anything maliciously. I wasn't purposefully trying to make his guys look bad. But that had been the result. And I hadn't even noticed what I'd done at the time. Joe had given me the benefit of the doubt that I hadn't meant to do the harm that I did to his guys, so he'd promised them he'd address the issue at a later time, and they trusted that he would. Hence his visit.

Joe's message to me was simple. Before you open your mouth and make an ass out of yourself, think for a minute how your words are going to be heard by the people that are busting their tails doing a hard job. Before you demoralize them with some thoughtless comments, take a minute, and think before you speak. I completely understood why he was there. And I absolutely respected how he let me understand for myself how what I had said had come across to his guys.

I admired Joe for coming to me and having done it in a completely calm way, while being blunt and not beating around the bush about what had happened. At the same time, as blunt as he was, he didn't make me feel like I was a bad guy. In fact, he offered up the thought that I hadn't intended the harm—that I had made an error in judgment, not an intentional slight. I became a huge Joe Santos fan that day.

I can't say that I never put my foot in my mouth on an ops call again, but that little coaching moment Joe gave me has stayed with me, and it's something I won't easily forget. I'm sure it wasn't easy for him to come and give me hard feedback. I'm sure that most people would have been uncomfortable doing it, but he had made a decision to bring me into his team and he valued me enough to want to make me a better leader and to learn from my mistakes. That took courage. And, he did it all in a way that made me realize what I had done, but I never felt like he resented me for it. Maybe he did, I don't know. But he didn't make me *feel* that way.

This is one of the things that really made Delta a special place to work. Its leaders, by and large, are successful in working out their issues peer-to-peer. That's what you do with family.

You give each other the respect of telling someone when you see them screw up. Then you pick them back up and tell them it's going to be okay. We all fail. It's part of the plan. In the end, it's all about how you pick up the pieces (uh-huh).

CHAPTER 8

Setting Course Correction

Out of every evil must come some good, it is said.
–C.E. Woolman

One of the lesser-known perks of working for an airline is that you get to fly for free. It's literally the sole reason why some people even *get* into the airline industry. For many of us, it becomes a reason to *stay* in the airline industry, especially when times get tough. Every carrier has slightly different rules on how the system works, but it's a near universal benefit of working in the industry. And you know what? It is as awesome as it sounds.

Now, realistically, you can make more money working in other industries. We all know that. And you can say to yourself that you could leave and go somewhere else and earn enough to cover the cost of taking whatever flights you'd want. But the reality is that you could never really justify paying for some of the trips that an airline employee might take, no matter how much extra money you might make.

I decided one day to take my son from Atlanta to Columbia, South Carolina, for an hour. He was two years old at the time. He loved airplanes. I figured on one lazy Saturday morning that he and I should have lunch in South Carolina. So, we went down to Hartsfield-Jackson International, caught a half-empty flight, and less than an hour later, we touched down in the tiny, little airport in Columbia. We ate lunch, waited for the next flight to Atlanta, and were home in time for an afternoon nap. That was a great day for my son and me.

I never would have paid for that trip. No reasonable person that values money in any way would pay for a trip like that. But an airline employee does that sort of trip all the time. You want to go to New York to catch a Broadway play and come back the next morning? Sure. Go to D.C. for the afternoon to see the Smithsonian and fly right back to sleep in your own bed that night? Yeah, why not? Hop on an open first-class seat you spotted to Seattle for the free meal and the movie and take the red eye back for the free breakfast? I've seen it done. Heck, someone told me they flew up to Boston to hand-deliver a wedding invitation to a friend because it was cheaper than buying a postage stamp! You'd never pay for a plane ticket to do any of that nonsense if you didn't work for an airline.

Working for a major air carrier certainly has its perks. However, any of us who have been in the industry for a long enough time will tell you that you have to be willing to be flexible with your plans. In fact, you'd better be willing to route yourself through some pretty creative paths to get from point A to point B. Airline employees travel on what we call stand-by priority. That means that if a flight doesn't sell out and there are unused seats, we get to use those seats to go wherever we want to go. For free. Anywhere in the world that our company flies. Which usually includes anywhere that our code share partners fly too!

So, the risk is that if a flight gets sold out, or if there is a flight cancellation in a connecting market and the airline needs to make last-minute accommodations for paying passengers, you can find yourself getting bumped for as long as it takes to get some open seats for you to use. It can be frustrating at times, but it can be the best feeling in the world when you get the last seat on the plane, you see the doors close and you're on board! It's an adventure every time.

Those of us who have become experts at what we call "non-revenue stand-by" flying have learned a valuable life lesson: you have to be open to last-minute course corrections. For example, you might be trying to fly from LGA (New York) to LAX (Los Angeles). You get to the airport and, all of a sudden, a flight gets cancelled from LGA to SFO (San Francisco) and the airline needs to divert passengers to LAX on any available unsold seat they had on that flight. If you were on stand-by for that LGA-LAX flight, then congratulations, you just got bumped.

Those of us who are in-the-know will immediately look at which other airports offer service to LAX that also service LGA to identify a secondary route to our destination. For instance, I might look at another hub that LGA flies to, such as ATL (Atlanta) or SLC (Salt Lake City). Or, if I know there are a bunch of other stand-by passengers who out-rank me in seniority, I might look, instead, at the obscure routes that have bailed me out in the past, such as STL (St. Louis), MCI (Kansas City), or IAH (Houston). We all have our primary and secondary back-up favorites to try. I've even met some folks that will go from JFK (New York) to CDG (Paris, France) just to get back to ATL. You begin to think very differently about how to travel when flying is free.

One great thing about being a frequent, non-revenue stand-by traveler is that it really teaches you about decision making. You constantly have to risk-rate your chances of getting on each flight based on the information that you see updated every few minutes. These days, things move so fluidly that the number of seats available can change all the way up to when the gate agent closes the doors. But the airline gives its employees fantastic, real-time information so they can see the changes as they are happening.

My family has got used to having to make quick decisions at the last minute, and we all mentally prepare for it in advance when we're planning to fly. If ATL to SFO is looking too tight for comfort, for example, and there is a flight that departs ten minutes sooner to SMF (Sacramento) that's wide open, we've already weighed the pros and cons of flying there and renting a car to get to SFO instead. We have been forced to make decisions like that so many times that it has made us comfortable with not being married to our initial plans and switching course (quite literally) to go with a less risky plan.

There are a couple of really good side benefits to the company for allowing this wonderful, stand-by travel perk. For starters, this is a guaranteed way to make sure that your airline employees understand and appreciate the product you're offering to your customers. If you don't use the product that your company sells, you will have no idea how to relate to your customers, which is bad. As a result, incentivizing your employees to constantly use the product to stay current is good.

Another benefit to the company is that all of the employees understand your route structure, the airports, and the logistics in getting between cities, and this also makes for a more educated employee base. And you don't have to pay them to learn all of this—they happily do it for free! And they teach their kids, who also become great future potential airline employees. I've hired a whole bunch of people who grew up in airline families: they come in already knowing about all of the flight logistics. And they're already hooked on flying stand-by, so they don't leave. It's great!

In my view, the biggest benefit to the airline in having their employees participate in this wild gambling game called stand-by travel is that you automatically expose your employees to the idea of being open to course correction. This is a critical element in business and in leadership, no matter which industry you work in. If you can help people learn that they are not obliged to plough on through the first plan they come up with, then you've trained your entire employee base on how to make risk-reward–based decisions about switching over to a Plan B. Or Plan C, if necessary.

To give you an idea on how effectively the typical airline employee can use their stand-by travel privileges to get to where they want to go, I'll give you some of my stats. Between my parents, my wife, my kids, and I, there have been about 1,150 successful stand-by boardings over the past two decades (I just looked it up in our system). The number of individual flight legs where any one of us purchased a ticket due to not being able to get on an airplane is three[23]. I estimate we use our flight benefits about as much as the average airline employee. I also estimate that I'm about average or worse at finding creative routes. Still, a success ratio of 1,150:3 is pretty dang good.

I credit a lot of success that I've had not only in stand-by travel but also in life and in business to having had to learn how to make lots of decisions, quickly, about how to get from point A to point B. It's taught me to be open to changing the plan when I see the current one isn't going to work. You get forced to evaluate risks, cut bait on your first route, and course correct on the fly to make it to where you want to go. In business, and in life, this is a crucial skill. As a leader, it'll make or break you.

There's a ton of different things that can and will go wrong with your plans in the business world. Sometimes it'll just be bad execution by you or someone that's working for you. When it's

23 I got stuck in Seattle during July of 2015 with two of my kids. I had decided to go there when flights out of SFO were starting to look bleak, and I was chasing a red-eye flight to ATL that had 40 seats left at the time I left SFO. Every one of those seats disappeared within the next twelve hours, and I had to carry two children, who were both asleep, from the terminal to a hotel in the wee hours of the morning. I broke down when I got to the hotel and bought tickets for the three of us. It was the only time I ever bought a ticket for my family or me while working at Delta.

poor execution and there's nothing wrong with the plan itself, then you do some coaching, pick up the pieces, and move on to get back on the plan. However, when the situation makes it clear that the plan is broken, you've got to course correct.

Course correction can just mean that you have to go back and re-draw up your plan. Maybe it's a slight tweak and not a complete redo. Sometimes you look at all the things you could possibly do, and you find out that there is no plan that will work. Then you need to reconsider making a change to the goal itself. That's also a course correction. Sometimes you dig deeper and figure out that it's not just the goal, but your entire vision that isn't right. You have to be open to each of those possibilities, no matter how much you once believed in them.

One of the most common things that a leader faces is making decisions about what to do when things are going wrong. If you've done a good job hiring people who are generally good, then you've probably got to sit down and look at your plan, and at how you are using those good people. Obviously, if you've hired poorly, there's not a hell of a lot that you're going to be able to do to correct that, other than to get busy moving that problem employee out the door.

If you think that's a crass way to think about things, you're right—but it doesn't change basic facts. Some people just make lousy employees. That's not your fault. It's not your company's fault. Your shareholders are not looking to you to be a charity for these people, either. And guess what? Your other employees, who are working around the people that are bad at their job, don't appreciate the fact that you can't stomach the idea of dealing with the problem either.

In fact, the people that tend to suffer the most from your inability to course correct or your inability to hire the right employees and let go of those that aren't are the people you hired who are actually good! I have become an ardent believer in the old adage, "Hire quick, but fire quicker"! If you don't do this, you'll be sorry you didn't as the people you actually value on the team start to leave your team, one by one, out of frustration.

The good news is that most people aren't bad employees. I'm not any better than anyone else at selecting good candidates to hire. I've had to personally hire over 100 employees in the last decade from full-time employees and cooperative students (interns) to contractors. Even with a lot of experience in hiring, I've not hired any better than my peers (some of whom have much less experience). I've had to let about 20% of all of the people I've hired go at some point. That's actually a pretty big percentage, so that tells you I'm not a perfect judge of character. But it also tells you that a much bigger percentage of people (the 80% that work out) end up doing pretty well at their job.

The bad news is that some leaders have spent decades in leadership roles and *never* fired anyone. Do you think they're really that much better at hiring good people than the rest of us? And, if the good people are the ones that tend to leave groups that have bad people in them, what percentage of *good* people remain in those groups after a couple of decades of zero house cleaning? Pretty low, from my experience.

You must correct your *own* mistakes first. You're going to screw up somewhere between 10% and 20% of the time when you hire people. Quickly fix the mistakes you made. Don't let your own mistakes fester any longer than it takes to give people a fair chance to prove themselves. Be fair but be quick with those moves when you need to make them.

So, what do you do about the poor execution of a plan when you've only got good employees left on the team when you've had to pick up the pieces too many times, but you know that it isn't because they aren't the right people? Well, the other thing that you could have screwed up is to have assigned the wrong people to the wrong assignments. This is where leading a team becomes a little bit of an art.

First of all, you have to know everyone on your team. You have to figure out, from their successes, what they do well. And you have to pay a lot of attention to figure out, from their failures, what they don't do well. You have to constantly look at changing your lineup so that you are always playing to the strengths of the team. You may have several people on your team who all have the same exact title. If you give them each exactly the same work because of this, you may not do well as a leader. Not all people are created with equal skills. Don't pretend that they are robots. They are human beings, and they have many flaws—just like you. Don't keep setting up your team for failure. Use them where they will do well!

When I took over the 24-7 Liaison Engineering team, I inherited 22 engineers: 13 full-time employees, three contractors, and six cooperative students from various universities across the Southeast. The team took care of everything from the pre-merger Delta fleet types that were out flying, to aircraft from any fleet type whenever they came into the Atlanta Jet Base for a scheduled visit to the hangar bays. This group hadn't gone through much change since I had started at Delta. The airline had, though.

It wasn't that you literally had the same people in the Atlanta Liaison team for all of those years. In fact, the vast majority of engineers who were hired into that group only stuck around for two or three years. Rotating between day shift, evening shift, and midnight shift every six weeks is a hard thing to do for an extended period of time. It's good for young people straight out of school and for people who like to sign up for permanent evening or midnight duties if they don't have a young family. But as soon as people start to settle down, it stops working for most people.

About the only thing that had remained constant through the previous 15 years had been a couple of the lead engineers. They were the ones on permanent shift assignments. And their general manager, Tony Muller (my boss), had been in charge of the team for nearly 20 years. As a result, it's not a huge surprise that the group hadn't really gone through huge fundamental changes. The most senior engineers—who trained all the new engineers—and the leadership in charge—who gave direction to the leads—were mostly the same people who had been there for a long time.

The benefit of these people having been able to anchor the group for all those years is that the team had built up a healthy knowledge base for everything in which those engineers and leaders had expertise. Tony was a really strong structures engineer[24] who had started his career at McDonnell Douglas in Southern California supporting the C-17 manufacturing line. He had a lot of pride in his analysis capabilities on sheet metal repairs and, naturally, he built his lead engineers into a really strong, structural analysis team. They could handle some truly complicated sheet metal repairs to wing, fuselage, or empennage structure.

The problem came when the team got handed anything that wasn't a piece of structure or when it wasn't made out of metal. Back in the day, when Tony had come on board and the Liaison Engineering team received requests from the Line Maintenance crews for help, the help they typically needed was to get repair designs drafted up for (mostly) metallic structure. In the 1990s and early 2000s, the application of aviation maintenance rules was a bit different from today, so the vast majority of other ATA subjects, such as cabin interiors issues and electrical systems, were dispositioned by the FAA-licensed mechanic right there on location. Things started to change with regulatory oversight by the late 2000s, and the business hadn't quite yet adjusted to it at the time that I came on the scene.

The result was that we started getting flooded with types of requests that had nothing to do with calculating tension strength, compression strength, and moments of inertia on sheet metal cross sections. When these other ATA subjects came in, there was very little knowledge within the team on those types of issues. A couple of the leads, who had been there a long time, were good at solving some of those other problems, but the

---

24 Tony would later become the Chief Engineer at Delta Air Lines

young engineers who had been trained exclusively by structures experts were not comfortable with those requests.

Being the safety-conscious company Delta is, people are taught that if they don't know the answer, they shouldn't pretend to know it: always err on the side of safety. These engineers were very safety conscious and had been trained to never sign off on anything they didn't understand. When something came their way that was beyond their expertise, they punted it on to someone else who was knowledgeable in that ATA chapter's subject matter. Sometimes this meant that they'd send a telex off to Boeing asking them to use their expertise as the original equipment manufacturer (OEM) to help offer an acceptable safe repair to whatever the problem was that the Delta team couldn't solve on their own.

The problem with sending telex messages to the OEM is that a lot of time goes by before you get a response. Sending a message with all the details necessary to accurately convey the technical details of an aircraft system that isn't functioning properly and getting a final answer back from the OEM's engineering department can take hours. You're playing a four-man game of telephone between the line mechanic, the MCC, the liaison engineer, and the OEM engineer who is 2,600 miles away (and who has a lot of other airlines calling with other problems). It took hours, even days sometimes, to get answers.

Delta Maintenance groups got sick and tired of hearing from the young Delta Liaison team that, "We've got to go to Boeing for this one." That was like hearing a death sentence verdict for the next ten flights that their aircraft needed to fly. It started to get to the point where the MCC would start calling the director of engineering in the middle of the night to complain that they weren't able to get in touch with a single engineer in the whole company that could guide them through what they needed to do about a damaged placard (true story).

I had done a ten-year stint as a support engineer in the composite repair shop at the start of my career. I liked sheet metal, and I had a reasonable amount of experience with repairing metallic structures, but my strengths have always been with bonded structures[25]. Given that I had also recently served some time managing Delta's Cabin Ops Engineering team, Tony thought I might be able to help him do some course correction with his team. I begrudgingly agreed.

It wasn't that I was worried about not having a lot of good people on this new team I was joining. In fact, Tony and the team had done a wonderful job hiring smart engineers. I was the dumbest one on the team, by far. From top to bottom, this group of engineers was brilliant— full of guys and gals that had graduated in the top of their class at some very fine institutions. The only problem was that they only specialized in one thing as a group.

Aside from the couple of guys on the team who were actually interested in all of the other things that make airplanes work, the bulk of the team had come to this group for one thing:

---

25 I drafted the lion's share of the Society of Automotive Engineers (SAE) Aerospace Information Report (AIR) 6291, which was titled, "Guidelines for Repair Process Evaluation of Aluminum Bonded Structure" and was Chairman of the SAE's Commercial Aircraft Composite Repair Committee's (CACRC) Airworthiness Task Group from 2011-2012, so I had a little bit of street credibility in the non-traditional metallic structures world.

to learn airframe repair. Mechanical or hydraulic systems didn't get them out of bed in the morning. They didn't find electrical engineering fascinating. Pneumatics was not their passion. It was all about that aluminum fuselage, the wing-box, the pylon, the floor structure, and that tail.

Tony also recognized, as I did, that we were about to start buying airplanes that were going to be made from that black metal called "carbon fiber." Boeing and Airbus were both rolling out all composite fuselage aircraft, and it was becoming clearer that metal was on the way out for next generation designs. So, we had to make some major changes in order to morph into a problem-solving group rather than just a group of metallic structural repair engineers.

I'll be honest - the first year and a half I was in my new role was a train wreck. I'd like to tell you that I had fun and that I inspired the team to want to come in every day to learn how to solve new and interesting problems. But I can't do that. Nothing that I tried that first year worked. My team hated the new direction we were heading. A few of them told me almost daily that they didn't have the right training to undertake the new type of work we were assuming. We didn't have enough people. Our office was run-down and outdated. And we had way too many phone calls coming in from all over the world requesting help with AOS aircraft to do anything but tread water.

The one saving grace was that in the first three months on the job, I had been successful in getting top management to allow me to hire some of the additional engineers Tony and I had requested who were badly needed. We had 16 degreed engineers on staff, so I asked for another eight. That number came out of the analysis that Tony and I did that clearly showed that the group was going to soon drown from all of the growth the fleet was undergoing. We calculated the number of bodies we needed to get to a point where we could meet our turn-time goals and the math made sense to our superiors.

The hangar management team was completely supportive of our business case, as they always played second fiddle to requests coming in from active AOS aircraft on the line. Some of it was due to lucky timing, but I got every one of those eight positions approved. It went up the chain all the way to Richard Anderson (probably buried in a stack of 200 other things on the docket), and he signed off on it.

If you've ever tried to go out and hire a bunch of people all at once and do it in a very short period of time, then you may already know what happened next. In the scramble to get in more help, I hired in a couple of engineers who weren't stellar. But, as luck would have it, most of the eight I had hired were actually pretty solid. One thing that was good was that I knew not to sell the idea that the new hires were coming in to focus on developing structural repair designs. They came in with the expectation that it was a true aircraft repair job they were bidding on—not just sheet metal and structures.

As I started to bring these new people in, I immediately started to see the attrition that the previous managers had all had to deal with. Within a month, I had the first engineer come knocking on my office door to hand in his two-week notice. He was going to be heading off to the engine repair shops. He wasn't really interested in doing the type of work that I needed them to focus on, and he was going to a normal Monday through Friday day-shift position. I completely understood, so I wished him well, and we shook hands.

A couple of months later, one of the contract engineers that I had interviewed for one of those eight full-time slots came to me and gave me an ultimatum. He demanded more pay. I declined. He left. Then, just a couple months after that, one of the evening shift engineers came to me and let me know that she had accepted a position with another airline and was heading out within the month. She also wasn't enjoying the new work that I had brought into the group, and I know that factored into her decision to leave. The one that added insult to injury was the co-op student who told me that he decided to call it quits after just one semester despite the fact that they are required to do three to get credit for the program. Things felt like they were running off the rails at this point.

For every employee who left I had to find another one to replace them. And that meant I had to get a couple of my lead engineers to dedicate time to interviewing three or four new candidates with me for each position we needed to fill. It was a constant barrage of candidates, interview forms, HR offer letters, new-hire training, and first-day lunches. And of course, it was also a constant process of collecting people's badges, cleaning up used cubicles, taking people to goodbye lunches, and replacing nameplates.

In less than a year, the group looked absolutely nothing like the one that I had inherited. Heck, even the office space itself was completely different. I had managed to horse-trade my way into getting it totally rebuilt in month six. I had some real estate that another team wanted. So, I made a deal.

I told them I'd give up part of our space if we could share a conference room in the space between our two office areas—if they would use part of their build-out budget to rebuild our whole Liaison office, as well. They had actually overestimated the budget for their renovation, so they had over $200,000 more than they needed. It worked out! We finally got a renovation to our dilapidated office after over 20 years. And I even got a chance to build a small kitchenette, complete with a full-sized fridge, double sink, microwave oven, and a Keurig coffee maker that we were able to hook up directly into the incoming tap water supply lines!

One element of course correction is repurposing what you have. Now that I had been able to give the physical office space a facelift, it was time to figure out how to reuse the talent that we had in the group that hadn't yet bailed out on me. I figured that anyone who was still there at that point was at least willing to work with me toward the vision we were setting out to achieve. Not all of them were completely on board yet, but they hadn't all left. Of the original 16, 11 were still around after that first year had passed.

Since I had lost five engineers that year, I had to bring in someone to fill each of those slots in addition to the eight new slots. That means 13 new engineers were hired into my new system, working side-by-side with the 11 I had inherited. We had a good mix of engineers with extensive aviation experience along with some new talent right out of college, and in between there were some journeymen with three to five years under their belt.

The ones I had hired were on board with the direction I had set. They had to be—that's the vision I presented to them when I hired them, and it was a condition of their employment that they support my vision. Of the 11 from the old guard, six of them actually liked getting exposure to the different aircraft systems that we were now supporting. However, the other five really did not. They loved their sheet metal repairs. But they were also really damned good at it, so there had to be a way to get everyone focused on their strengths and their passions.

One of our up-and-coming engineers, Brad Hanson, suggested a better way to use everyone to their strengths and comfort levels. He was one of the team members who regularly gave me feedback about what I was doing to the team and how I had everything wrong. He was not thrilled about any of it. But he was, arguably, the best engineer on the team at his experience level. He was about five or six years out of college at that time. He was one of my go-to engineers for anything really complicated that needed to be done right and be done now. And he was willing to do lots of overtime and on-site travel to wherever the airplane was to get it done. He was even willing to regularly go to Detroit, which really made him special!

He gave me one of the best ideas that we ever implemented in that Liaison group. He pointed out that there were several engineers who were really passionate about sheet metal structures repairs. He also pointed out to me that almost 100% of the work that came in from the scheduled hangar visits in Atlanta was structures-related repair requests. We knew that it took about six, fully dedicated heads to support the hangar work that was routinely coming into our office. We also knew that there were at least five engineers who only wanted to do the complicated sheet metal repair development work. And we both knew we could easily find one more who could be happy focusing on that type of work.

The question Brad asked me was, "Why don't we split the group into two teams?" His idea was that one team would be totally dedicated to the structures requests that came in from the hangar. The other team would do nothing but focus on the line requests, which could be any issue under the sun, including the occasional structural repair request. It was pretty simple. And it seemed like it would kill two birds with one stone: we could get all of the engineers doing what suited them best and made them happiest and, at the same time, get the airline what it needed to support the line and the hangar.

I told Brad I'd be willing to do it if he could organize the team that would be signing up to support the hangar requests. And, if he could figure out a schedule throughout the week to get true 24-7 coverage to support it, I'd be willing to make it a permanent arrangement for the team. If you do the math on that, it's actually not really possible to get the coverage, considering you have to factor in vacation requests. But Brad came back to me a few days later having negotiated some "dark" periods with the hangar management team. Actually, he had asked one of the newer engineers, Ivana Gonzalez[26], to do this negotiation with the hangar - she was the one he credits with coming up

26 Ivana will surely become an officer of the company if she chooses to stay on with Delta for 15 or more years. If not, I'll be saddened, because that means she will have left Delta to become a star at some other company less deserving. She is fearless and is extremely sharp - I am happy to take credit for hiring her into Delta! We also found her through the annual Society of Hispanic Professional Engineers (SHPE) conference as a co-op student while she was attending Georgia Tech, so that's another success story for our recruiting strategy outlined later in the Epilogue.

with the schedule that he was proposing. This impressed me, as he was already getting his team together to create plans and negotiate those plans with the customer, which are things that leaders naturally do without being asked.

He explained to me that I didn't really *need* full 24-7 coverage. There were gaps that could be managed. For example, between 2:00 a.m. and noon on Sundays, we could take a small break. Hangar aircraft could stand to go a 10-hour period on the weekends during non-peak times with a gap in coverage. The hangar management team agreed. So, I signed it off.

There were some hiccups with the schedule, but the team managed to work with Brad to get them corrected as they came up. The team was incentivized to make it work, so it worked. They knew that if I heard about problems within the team, I'd attempt to fix them myself. And they didn't want that. They wanted their autonomy, and they didn't want to risk having to go back to line-support duties and have to repair designs for curtains and doilies.

It took some time to get the plan totally on course. I had a lot of late nights, and there were some extremely early mornings. There were growing pains over the weekends with the new leads I had hired in. It was hard. At that early point, I hated it most of the time. But I wouldn't trade that experience for anything. In the end, we did get over the hump, and my job, after a couple years, actually became a little boring. When things started to finally click, there was the occasional drama, but I had the system on autopilot most of the time from there on out.

Looking to the long-term, I created a junior manager role for Brad. He had done a great job coming up with a way for us to correct our course when my original plans weren't working for the team. He helped me hang on to some engineers who probably would have left to look for better opportunities had we not carved out that little dedicated hangar-support team.

I was able to set up the same type of role for one of the other lead engineers to manage the schedule and day-to-day personnel management on the line-support teams. We built a structure with a lead engineer, a senior engineer, an entry-level engineer, and a co-op engineer on each of the six shifts that rotated through the week. This allowed people to take vacations and still have adequate coverage with someone on-shift that had at least three years' experience. And they all knew they could wake me up if they needed help making decisions. At first, they often did this. Sometimes it was just because they thought it was funny. But over time, my sleep got better. By the end of my three years there, I was sleeping like a baby.

When I left the group, I had a well-oiled machine that didn't need me. In fact, when I ultimately did leave for my next job, Tony eliminated my position altogether. He gave the line-support team to the incoming manager and Brad rolled in underneath one of his other managers—a peer of mine. It was one of those times where I really did work my way out of a job. And it was everything I thought it should be.

Course correction can be the toughest thing to commit to. In many ways, it's admitting the fact that there has been a failure. And since you are the leader, it was, ultimately, *your* failure. But if you allow yourself to have the occasional failure, just like you allow the people on your team to fail so they learn and get better, you'll start to accept the need to change the plan and get back on track to meet your goals. And when you accept the need to change, you'll look for chances to make those badly needed changes. This is the one thing that you absolutely cannot fail to do. Master this art, and there's no limit to where you can go.

CHAPTER 9

Recognizing Victory

Goodwill pays dividend...and goodwill is an asset that won't show up on the balance sheet but is the most important factor in operating a successful airline.
–C.E. Woolman

Nine billion one hundred fifty-five million dollars. Let's write that differently: $9,155,000,000. Damn, that's a lot of zeroes. That's the amount of bonus money that went out to all frontline employees and frontline managers during my last ten years at Delta Air Lines. It was part of the profit-share plan that Delta had put into place to reward all of those employees who had stuck it out during bankruptcy and rebuilt Delta into the perennial commercial airline juggernaut that it became in the 2010s. Even when you spread that out over about 90,000 employees, that's still a life-changing amount of money for a lot of people. It paid for a lot of new cars, new boats, new houses, and college tuition payments for a lot of kids.

There has never been a larger distribution of corporate wealth in the history of company profit-share programs. Actually, I've always said that, but I don't even know how to look up stats on that to verify its accuracy. Either way, it's a ridiculously large number—$9,155,000,000. It doesn't even look like a real number when you write it out. Over any single ten-year period, it has to be a record, right? I know the $1.6 billion that we paid out for 2019 was a world record. The internet says it's so. I'm going to keep saying it until someone proves I'm wrong!

Rewind about 13 years. In 2007 we were coming off our relighting ceremony on the top of the hangar for the Fly Delta Jets sign. The one that we had shut off to save money after 9/11 when we were losing money hand over fist. We were just about to officially emerge from Chapter 11 bankruptcy. Our managers all sat us down some time in April of that year and explained how we were going to share in the success of the airline going forward. The leadership team had just announced this new profit-share program. And every single frontline employee in the company was eligible to reap the rewards.

It sounded nice and all. But we hadn't actually made a profit in any single year since I had joined the company, so I kind of wrote it off as a whole lot of hot air. We were told, however, that we would all receive something like 10% of all profits up to $2 billion and then 20% of all profits greater than that[27]. I

27 Don't quote me on this—it's been a while, and I'm going completely off of memory. The profit share plan has changed a few times in the last decade, and I can't keep it straight anymore.

remember thinking that we'd never, ever, reach the $2-billion mark, so assumed it was pointless even having that 20% clause in there. They just seemed like fantasy numbers. We'd been losing more money than that every year, so even making one dollar profit seemed like a goal we'd dance in the street for.

In 2007, riding off of the extremely high emotional energy we had from our escape from bankruptcy, we eked out a pretty nice profit, which earned a profit-share payout of $158,000,000 to be shared among all of us front line employees on Valentine's Day in 2008. Not bad. We were pretty shocked about that. Right out of the gate this little profit-share thing was already paying off. We all were issued some company stock that year, which, for a change, was worth more than zero dollars, unlike the shares we had in our 401(k) plans after we filed for bankruptcy. It was a great start to this new emerging airline.

We were all brought back down to earth in 2008 and 2009 when we lost $503,000,000 and $1,200,000,000, respectively. "Great," I remember thinking. "Back to reality." No profit share for both of those years, obviously. And the stock hit low single digits—not a good follow-up to our great start. If you remember, that was around the time of the great collapse of the financial markets. We were heavily leveraged with fuel hedges and had been belly-bumping and high-fiving each other as it looked like oil prices would never stop rising. This was a highly counterintuitive thing for an airline to hope for since we normally *lost* money when fuel costs increased. But then the bottom fell out of the oil market, and we were losing money hand over fist, again—this time because fuel had *dropped*!

Richard Anderson and Ed Bastian made some pretty drastic course corrections with fuel strategies after 2008. (In fact, as a result of this disaster, they went on to buy an oil refinery in 2012 to try to control the crack spread.) When our hedging contracts expired and the economy started to get back on its feet, we started making money again. In fact, we didn't just start making money, we started making a whole *lot* of money.

We got to a point in the early part of the last decade where we started stringing together record profits, and we were making it a game to see how much we could make. On profit-share day in February of 2014, we were celebrating over a half a billion in profit share from $2.7 billion in net income from our 2013 performance. That was the first time we ever made it into that 20% zone I have found so implausible back in 2007. Someone at Delta made some T-shirts that people started wearing in late January of 2014 that simply said $3B on the front. That was our new goal for the current year. Around the company, folks started campaigning to surpass $3 billion in net income for 2014.

The general managers and directors were all wearing these ridiculous red $3B T-shirts to one of our operations meetings one Friday, and I remember thinking how silly it seemed. I figured we should be shooting for something more like $4B. After all, we'd gone from $1 billion profit in 2012 to $2.7 billion in 2013. Why not go for broke and challenge ourselves for another measly 50 percent increase in profit? Apparently, the rest of the frontline workers agreed. They all responded by torching the previous record and posted a performance that yielded a $4.5 billion profit!

And each year, the bonus checks kept rolling in, getting bigger and bigger and bigger each year. Every year, I'd hear frontline guys using the profit-share reference in everyday conversation. You'd tell a guy in the MCC that you didn't have time to give him a solution for an aircraft that had to be moved from Johannesburg to JFK. You'd get responses like, "Hey man, we lose that flight and that's money right out of our pockets on profit-share day." It was a big thing on everyone's mind. When the company won big, we all won big. When the company lost, that was *our* money we had just lost. It forced us to think about things a lot differently. Suddenly, this was *our* business, and we were all working for each other. We weren't just employees of a company. We were stakeholders in a huge joint venture.

Delta had been smart to create that scheme in the spring of 2007. Our leaders had known that it would take some years for it to really change our culture, but they had also correctly guessed that, once we got addicted to the results of success, we'd keep pushing ourselves to outdo ourselves, year after year.

Every year, we threw ourselves one big party on February 14. We allowed ourselves to spike the football in the end zone one day of the year. And then, on February 15, we forgot about last year, and focused on how we were going to beat last year's record and set a new one.

That is, legitimately, how we approached coming into work every day. We constantly asked ourselves, "How are we going to beat last year?" It was important to us. Hell, it was important to our spouses, our kids, our churches, and communities. Everyone in the entire Atlanta airport business community benefitted from it and celebrated our wins every year—and we did it together.

It's genius. When the team is able to recognize that the company winning means that *they* win, too, it becomes important to them to make that win happen again and again. If the company's victory is easily understood to be *the team's* victory, as a leadership team, you've solved the most important part of the puzzle: you've got your team fully invested in the results of your business. And congratulations, because now you have hundreds, thousands, or even tens of thousands in our case, of highly motivated business stakeholders who will think of the next big idea to make *you* more money. And buckle up—you're going to be breaking some records!

I've mentioned the quotation I kept on my desk all those years: "There is no limit to what a man can do or where he can go if he doesn't mind who gets credit." Yes, Ronald Reagan did have it on his desk when he was president in the 1980s, but he wasn't the one that coined the phrase. In fact, it was Robert W. Woodruff, president of the Atlanta-based Coca-Cola Company from 1923 to 1954. And if you understand it and put it into practice, you'll unleash the last and, perhaps, the most valuable principle of leadership that you need to learn.

You've got to remember: your people are damned smart. That's why you hired them. If you didn't hire people who were smarter than you, then you didn't do a very good job hiring. So, since they're better at doing stuff than you are, then any victories are really all about them. They're the ones that really did the work. So, make sure that you recognize the victory that *they* achieved, for crying out loud!

One thing Richard Anderson and Ed Bastian never did was get up on a stage on Valentine's Day—our profit share celebration day—and spout off about all of the great things *they* had done as wonderful leaders and visionaries at Delta Air Lines[28]. Yes, we all knew the incredible role they had played. But they were smart enough to make that day all about *us* and what *we* did. And they taught us to make sure that *we*, as frontline leaders, made it all about what our *team* did. This was the epitome of what that plaque on my desk said. And how appropriate it was that it was the concept of one Atlanta-based company that was using the adage made famous by another Atlanta legend to achieve such great success.

When success happens, if it has anything at all to do with what *you* have done as a leader, it's that you hired good people and taught them how you wanted them to achieve your vision. In fact, when you sit down and look at what *you've* really done, it boils down to some basic stuff.

After you hired everyone, all you did was come up with a small vision and used your mediocre style to sell it to the team. *They* were the ones that really helped you figure out good goals. *They* came up with the plan with you that ended up working. Yes, you did regurgitate that plan to the whole team. Sure,

28 Contrast Richard and Ed's message to us with what Doug Parker, American Airlines' CEO, said in 2014 when asked about his thoughts of profit sharing: "It's just not the right way to pay 100,000 employees that don't have that much impact on the daily profits." Boy, I thank God every day that Doug's plan to take over Delta in 2006 failed!

you let them fail a little bit—congratulations for that bit of hard work of letting people fall down on their face. Then you picked them back up and said some reassuring things along the way. Yeah, okay, so you also fixed a few minor details in the plan that were—let's face it—somewhat inconsequential. Good job! Give yourself a medal for that, if it makes you feel better.

I'm being a bit facetious here, but in the end, you know what? *They* did the dang work that led you to the success you had. You're just the coach. Is it the coaches that you typically see rushing the field after the World Series is over? Heck no. It's the players! They batted in the runs that won the game. They got the game-ending double play to seal the win. They struck out the batters in the sixth, seventh, and eight innings to protect the lead. Not you. Then, let them have the satisfaction of the win.

Winning is addictive. There's a reason that you have dynasties in sports. Whether it's the Yankees, the Patriots, the Crimson Tide, or the Golden State Warriors, the players all want to keep winning. That is, as long as they feel like it is *their* win. They win for *themselves*—not for someone else! As long as it is about *them*, they'll keep shooting for the *next* title, time and time again. As soon as it becomes about someone else, forget about it. It's for themselves and their families, not for you and yours. Always remember that.

The funniest thing about recognizing people for their success is that it actually doesn't need to be about money. Sure, money is awesome. It's a universal thing that people use as a reward for a job well done and to incentivize future successes. But the interesting thing about being humans is that we are social animals who really value being recognized for the great things that we do.

Early in 2019, I was given three little orange stickers by an old friend. I don't even remember why he gave them to me, but I ended up putting them in my coat pocket. They were circular with a little smiley face on them, and they had "Thank You," written on them. I forgot about them for a while. One day, at DFP, while the team was finishing up one of our first big in-house manufacturing projects for Delta's 767-400 fleet, I asked a team member, David Hausman[29], to make sure we would be on track to support a shipping date in late January for some parts that needed to get shipped out to Guangzhou, China.

A couple of days later, I asked David if we were on track to meet our shipment, and he surprised me by saying that he had got everything finished up the previous night. He told me he had stayed late to make sure that everything was in order so we could make our shipment on time. That made me very happy, so I told him how much I appreciated his efforts. He joked that I could thank him by forking out a couple of Benjamins.

That's when I reached into my pocket, in jest, to see what I had to offer him. I pulled out one of the three stickers I had

29 David would later, almost single-handedly, become responsible for DFP obtaining its repair station certificate under 14 CFR Part 145. I was a brief holder of an FAA repairman certificate under the DFP repair station.

forgotten about and ripped one of them off and handed it to David. He said, "Gee, thanks, Todd."

I told him, "You know, that's actually worth more than money. There's only three of those in existence, and I just gave one of them to you." David was not entirely amused by my token of gratitude and was about to chuck his prize into the trash when I insisted that he might want to hang onto that little token.

So, in an effort to embarrass him in front of his colleagues, I announced, loudly, to the entire office, "Everybody stop what you are doing and listen up! David, here, has earned the most prestigious award that I am able to bestow upon any DFP employee." I held up the bright orange sticker and announced to everyone present that there were only three of these left in the world and that I was awarding this great prize to their esteemed colleague. I peeled off the sticker and firmly fixed it to his computer monitor so every passer-by would see it and be amazed at his achievement for this great honor. I razzed David a little more, then went back to my office.

Later that week, one of my other employees did something that was praiseworthy, and I thought it would be funny to reenact a similar ceremony for her. I peeled off the second-to-last Thank You sticker and affixed it to her monitor. David, who was present for this second impromptu award ceremony, protested again, in jest. He said that this had cheapened his Thank You sticker's value and that now it was worth only half of its original monetary worth. I reminded him that I still had, yet another, sticker to give out and that he might do well to earn it.

A week later, I had a third teammate that I just had to recognize with my last Thank You sticker. She had just implemented a new learning management system for our little startup company, and I was really impressed with how she was able to do it in such a short amount of time and execute it so well. I was now out of stickers, and David seemed genuinely upset that I had given my last sticker to someone else, further cheapening his major award.

I was having too much fun with this stupid little sticker, so I went on the internet and found some more just like it. Once, again, I forgot about it for a few days. Then they arrived in the mail, and I had 100 new incentives to hand out. So, I started to look for some excuses to award them to people all around the office. The new stickers weren't exactly like the originals: they were a little bigger and were a slightly different shade of orange. I reassured David that his original sticker was still valued higher than these new ones. His was, after all, a first series collector's item, by now.

I passed out a couple from the new batch over the next couple of weeks. Again, I embarrassed every new recipient with the same ridiculous office-wide announcement. I told everyone present that I was bestowing the highest award with which I could possibly honor any DFP person. I played it entirely straight-faced but was smiling on the inside. I admit it, I was having too much fun.

But then something happened. People actually started to legitimately congratulate the recipients of these stupid little stickers. When I stopped everyone and announced a new "award winner," the whole office started to erupt in applause and congratulatory responses. I didn't think anything of it at first, but then I got a visit. Kevin Hillen, my quality manager[30], came into my office one day and was giving me some feedback. He told me, "You know, I can't quite understand how this has happened, but people on the team are really starting to try to do things to try to earn one of your little Thank You stickers."

I looked at Kevin and just laughed. "What?!" I replied. "That's ridiculous!" Kevin laughed, shook his head, and reassured me that it was true. Apparently, a lot of the guys on his team were really trying to go out of their way to think of ways they could earn one of those cheap little stickers. And Kevin wasn't the only one who came in to tell me this. My head trainer, Catherine Coleman[31], also confided that one of her intern's big goals for the semester was to do something noteworthy enough to earn one of my stickers before he went back to school the next semester.

I was absolutely taken aback. Why in the world would people be that incentivized to perform just to be given a little five-cent sticker that had been mass-produced in the millions in China? But I realized it really said something about human nature. It really doesn't matter what you do to recognize people for their achievements, apparently. The point is to simply

---

30 Kevin and David were both the ones that were responsible for us getting our IS9001 / AS9100 certification at DFP. But I found them, so I feel like I can share in the pride of their success.

31 Catherine, by the way, is awesome. Rick used to tell me all the time that she was my best hire at DFP, and I cannot disagree with that, which says a lot, because he and I both feel that I hired some really good people at DFP.

recognize them. And it doesn't matter what walk of life you belong to. Everyone who is human loves to be recognized.

It wasn't just frontline employees that felt a sense of honor in being recognized with the little orange stickers, either. I gave one to our president, Rick, one day for helping me out with something. I don't even remember what it was that he had done, but when I gave it to him, he actually knew what it was and was excited to receive it! I don't know how he knew, but apparently it was something that he'd seen displayed across the company on people's computer monitors, and it made him feel special that he had earned one from me. He stuck it on his wall and made a big deal about it to his leaders. I couldn't fathom it.

The point is this: never underestimate how good you can make people feel just by recognizing their little everyday successes. And it doesn't matter who you are—a frontline employee, a middle manager, or a president. Everyone likes to get recognized for the things they do that make them feel victorious. When they succeed, they want you to recognize it. And as long as you recognize the victory, they'll keep wanting to repeat it, over and over again.

And that's really all there is to it. Have a vision. Get people to buy into the vision with a little style. Work with your team to create logical goals to meet your vision and then get them to tell you a viable plan to meet those goals. Make sure you communicate the team's plan across your entire broader group, then sit back and let it fail or succeed on its own. Respond to the failures with smart coaching moments. Course-correct when needed. And reward the victory with recognition. Rinse and repeat, forever. That's all there is to being a leader.

EPILOGUE

People ask me every day why I decided to retire from Delta, especially when I tell them about how much I loved my experience there. To put things in perspective, though, I had been a part of several rebuilding building projects over the two decades that I was there. I was a part (albeit a small part) of rebuilding the company after 9/11 and the subsequent bankruptcy. Then, as a direct result of our emergence and growth within our industry, I rebuilt the cabin operations engineering support team in an effort to keep up with the massive demand to support the customer experience in the sky. Then I went on to rebuild the 24-hour support engineering structure in Atlanta while also physically rebuilding our office to help that growing fleet continue to fly more efficiently and more often than any of our competitors.

I left engineering to build a subsidiary company from scratch. While at DFP, we literally had completed three phases of building and rebuilding our facility layout in three short years and were about to go through a massive Phase 4 build right at the time that the coronavirus pandemic hit us. And then the world stopped functioning. After several months, it became apparent to me that we were going to have to rebuild the entire airline all over again, and our subsidiary too, as a result.

There's only so many times you can try to put the world back together before you have to go ahead and pass that task on to someone else. I feel like I've seen a full cycle of a great company clawing its way back from the dead, achieving success, creating a dynasty from that early success, and then realizing perpetual greatness like it had decades in the past, year after year. Then I witnessed the next major bump in the road, but this one was different from the last one.

When we went into bankruptcy, that was *our* fault. We were complacent, we stopped fighting, and the result from that was that we almost went out of business. I promised myself that if I ever started to feel like I didn't have that fighting spirit left inside of me, that would be the time when I would need to do something different. If I didn't, it would be *my* fault for repeating history.

I looked around me last year and saw that, despite the awful situation we were in, that there were a lot of good people in our company who were still fighting hard, making sacrifices for the team, keeping good spirits about the cards we had been dealt, and that made me feel good about Delta's future. I asked myself if I had the drive to be a part of another arduous rebuild project and, unfortunately, I didn't see myself having as much energy as the next generation of leaders will have.

I remember the dark days of bankruptcy as actually being a fun challenge, as a young, emerging leader. A lot of the old guard had left the company and they kind of handed over the reins to those of us who stuck it out. I loved having the chance to make my own mark on the company and set things up my own way. It was really rewarding seeing that I could establish policies, set up my own procedures for my own teams, and run it like a business the way I saw fit. That was enormously fun. It was incredibly hard work, too. I shed a lot of blood, sweat, and tears during that time.

Over a ten-year period in leadership, I had gotten to a point where I literally had done everything that I was really interested in doing at Delta. In fact, I really ran out of ideas of things I thought I'd like to build. And that's really what made me start to think about hanging up my hat, even before the pandemic hit us in 2020. I felt myself getting stale. I needed to find a new challenge and reinvent myself. Money wasn't motivating me anymore. Getting the next promotion didn't interest me. And I really didn't feel like I had fresh ideas to bring to the team anymore. It was just the right time for me to let someone else take over and find joy in putting their own mark on the company.

I've kept in touch with a lot of my old friends in the past few months since I left. I hear some of the enthusiasm coming back in their voices—similar to what I heard when we were emerging from bankruptcy 14 years ago. People are starting to see the light at the end of this COVID-19 tunnel and that tells me that Delta is going to come out of this thing, once again, as the strongest competitor in the airline business. I don't typically like to buy stock in individual companies. In fact, there are only five companies of which I choose to be a shareholder today[32]. Delta is one of them. I know that they will be more than fine.

A lot of people tried to tell me that it was a bad idea to go into the airline industry when I did. My mother, for years, thought I should look at doing something else. In all fairness, she had watched my dad's brother (Uncle Mike) be a part of a couple of airline failures. He had been with both Braniff and Eastern and went down with the ship both times. He had to wait nearly ten years to get back into the commercial airline pilot ranks when he was finally picked up by Continental. He caught the last wave up with them and got out on a high note.

What my parents didn't see that I had a chance to see every day was the spirit of the Delta people. I was never really concerned for Delta. The thought never occurred to me that we'd ever do anything but survive and thrive. I do admit that I never thought we would get to the heights we did. But that just goes to show you that you should never underestimate the people at Delta Air Lines. More importantly, never underestimate the power good leadership can have to create a culture like we have within the world's greatest airline!

On hiring leaders:

When they are hiring for management positions, far too many people make the mistake of gravitating to those candidates who are just really good at whatever job they were previously

32 I prefer to hold Exchange Traded Funds (ETF's) and mostly hold ETF's that track against the S&P500. If there is one thing that I'd recommend to any young investor is this - put as much money into the S&P 500 as you can for as long as you can and retire early.

doing. The idea that someone performing well as an individual contributor should be "rewarded" with an opportunity as a manager is a nice thought. But it is dead wrong. In war, that'll often get people killed. In business, it'll often set you back years. A proper reward for a job well done is a bonus check or an opportunity to be trusted with a larger or more critical project. Rewards should have no connection with putting someone in charge of other people, except when that person has actually shown that the act they are good at is managing people!

I've seen a lot of general managers and directors fail because they don't understand the difference between someone who has high technical aptitude for their job and another candidate who is a highly effective leader. Admittedly, not all great leaders make great business managers. However, if you take someone who is brilliant at their job but who has zero leadership skills, that person will automatically fail *every* time. Given the choice of blindly betting on a candidate who is obviously a sound leader with unknown business acumen versus going with someone who really knows the business but has no aptitude for leadership, I will take my chances with the one who can lead people every single time. At the very least, their chance of succeeding is greater than zero.

If you hire the leader, then even if they turn out to be a total flop when it comes to the specific thing you hired them to lead, you can usually try different line-ups within your broader team to play to their strengths once you learn what they are. I almost always have to go through three or four line-up changes each time I take on a new team until I get to a point where I've got all of the right people aligned with their strengths. Get the right people onboard first, then you can spend time later figuring out where everyone needs to sit on that bus. Get the wrong people on the bus, and it doesn't matter where anyone sits—nothing will work.

On recreating teams:

Another major problem I've seen some people in upper management make is when they bring in too many people that they knew from another life into a new organization. That usually does more harm than good. It becomes problematic because they tend to miss out on getting a fresh perspective from the team they are inheriting and continue rely on the same stale ideas they were using their former organizations. They also tend to miss out on growing future replacement leaders in the process, which is a double whammy!

In my last leadership role, I had a truly unique opportunity to build a team from scratch. When I was hired into the role, we were building a subsidiary organization from the ground up and my department literally had one person in it—me. Due to the nature of this subsidiary, there were practical obstacles to attracting any employees from our parent company[33]. So, I effectively couldn't hire anyone that I knew. More or less everyone I hired came from 63another company with whom

33 Anyone I would have worked with beforehand worked for our parent company. To hire into a subsidiary from the parent company, you would lose all of your seniority and the other benefits, such as 401K and flight benefits, were also less attractive. As a result, in the first three and a half years as we grew from zero to over 325 employees, only one of them came from our parent company!

I had never worked. In reality, it was a blessing. I didn't have to worry about loyalty to friends or letting emotions outweigh decisions about what I needed to do if things didn't work out the way I had hoped. More importantly, though, every idea from the team was fresh to me!

Sometimes we make the mistake of thinking that if we just try to rebuild the same team we had at another place or within a different department that we're going to repeat the success that we had previously achieved. The reality is that it is a zero-sum game. The more you try to "get the band back together," the less value you create for the future of your company.

On developing new leaders:

A common mistake I've seen continually hinder top management is when we laser-focus in on a specific individual and put unrealistic expectations on that individual's growth within a leadership team. It is good to find a diamond in the rough, and it is natural to want to see someone that you've nurtured continue to grow as a leader and climb the promotional ladder. What can be devastating for that emerging leader is to put excessively high hopes on them by constantly promoting them before they are ready. This can stunt their ability to organically grow and make their own mistakes along the way (which is how everyone learns).

Unfortunately, what happens the vast majority of the time is that bad things end up happening for the company and even worse things happen to the individual. From the company viewpoint, you've now put an inexperienced leader in a position where their failure ends up negatively affecting mission-critical goals. And when they do fail, it ends up hurting pretty bad. From the individual viewpoint, their direct reports start out resenting them for not having "paid their just dues." When you start out facing resentment, it's hard to get buy-in from the employee groups. Without buy-in, you don't get good ideas from the team. And without great ideas from the team, you are usually forced to make uneducated decisions which, no matter how good you are, eventually fail. Since you rose to the top too fast, when you fail, it is epic. Try shaking that stigma for the rest of your career!

People need time to grow into their positions. Growth happens over years, not months. If you really want to do someone a favor, give them an opportunity when they are ready. Counsel them to be patient before seeking the next promotion. If they threaten to leave because they aren't getting the next promotion soon enough, then they weren't really interested in your business anyway, so why would you fight for that?

On developing diverse leadership:

I know there is also a lot of pressure to get leaders in place in their organizations who are culturally diverse. We all want that to happen. It's critical that your organization reflect both your customer base as well as the people you want to hire from all over the world. And yes, it's the right thing to have as a goal. We've learned that an executive team that is only made up of middle-aged white men is not going to make your organization highly competitive or rich with different perspectives. I get all of that, but you aren't helping the overall mission by taking a diverse employee straight out of frontline management with a team of ten direct reports and converting them to a vice-president over 2,000 employees over the course of three to four years. That sets them up for a meteoric fall. And do you think that makes the next person with the same background want to take that same fall in the future? All leaders from all types of backgrounds need and deserve time to grow into their roles.

We spent a lot of time attending career fairs that highlighted diverse candidates who were either looking for internships or who were fresh out of college looking for their first entry-level positions. There are great events out there that are hosted by organizations like the Society of Women Engineers (SWE), the National Society of Black Engineers (NSBE), and the Society of Hispanic Professional Engineers (SHPE) and we loved attending them. It gave us the opportunity to find some of the nation's top talent, hire them, mentor them, and promote them when they were ready. It was a long-range investment in people, but it was a fantastic investment that paid off over the years within our engineering and planning organization.

Every year I looked forward to the NSBE conference, which was the event that I got most involved with. My favorite part of being involved with that organization was watching the people we hired in as interns and co-ops grow over their time with the company and watching as new leaders emerged. Eventually, the strategy we had implemented in our college hiring program started to make meaningful impact on the makeup of our teams. You cannot achieve anything like that by just elevating one or two diverse stand-outs and hoping that it will somehow turn you into a diverse company. You need to set up a way to ensure that you always have a perpetual pipeline of candidates from varying backgrounds to cement your culture of diversity. I am truly proud of the work we did to change our entry-level hiring strategy within the Tech Ops engineering departments. It was rewarding to be a part of the creation of the vision and then to help lead the team to execute the vision and to be able to clearly see the results over the years.

Like anything that is worth doing right, a leader needs to be extremely patient. If you do the right things, over a long period of time, your investments will pay off, and your company will be in the best possible position to perpetually make money. I have witnessed a lot of the mistakes above: the good news is that we've figured out a successful formula anyone can follow if they have the basic ability to lead people, along with the patience and discipline to follow the formula. Just like there is no get-rich-quick plan that works across the board, there's no set of things you can do in your business to fix major problems overnight. As with the airline industry I come from, most industries share the common trait of measuring improvement over months and years instead of days and weeks.

Be patient. Find the right people. Follow the steps to lay out the vision, pick the right style, think of good goals with your team, lay out your plan with them, and set the expectation for what "good" looks like. Then step back and try to let people do what you hired them to do. They're going to make some mistakes. Let them. Pick them back up, dust off the rubble, and help them figure out how to avoid making the same mistakes again. Then, watch as they learn how to succeed. Finally, help them celebrate their successes. With a little luck, they'll be able to develop their own vision, develop their own style, and start to figure out their own goals and plans without you needing to be there. That is how you grow the leaders of tomorrow.

ABOUT THE AUTHOR

Originally hailing from Alamo, California, Todd Michael Herrington now lives in the Atlanta metropolitan area with his beloved wife, Catherine, and children (Charlie, Evelyn and Sylvia). He has two little angels in heaven (Lillian and Bridget) who watch over him every day. Receiving a Bachelor of Science degree in Mechanical Engineering from the Georgia Institute of Technology in 2001 (and graduating near the bottom of his class), he subsequently worked in commercial aviation for nearly twenty years serving in roles across several engineering disciplines, project management, as well as quality and safety. He is a proud founder of Delta Flight Products, LLC - one of the most ambitious subsidiary organizations that was ever founded in the commercial aviation industry.

Todd's passions, outside of spending time with his family, include teaching religious education to middle school students at his local parish, coaching youth baseball and softball, writing, and enjoying well-crafted, American distilled whiskey. He's still not sure what he wants to be when he grows up, but whatever it is, he's always going to remember the valuable lessons he learned while working for the greatest company on the planet.

STAY TUNED
NEW READ COMING SOON

BECOMING A PHOENIX

REBUILD AND RISE UP OUT OF THE ASHES

PREFACE

I love rebuilding things. As a kid, I used to take everything apart that I could get my hands on. Sometimes I even managed to put those things back together again in working order. As an engineer, it's programmed into my DNA – to break a component down, see what makes it work (or fail), and then figure out how to put it all back the way I found it (or maybe even a little bit better). My grandfather became a mechanic after the war ended. His garage was a collection of tools from several decades and there was nothing he couldn't put back together. My dad always did his own maintenance on his cars and boats and I remember holding his tools while he worked under the hood, learning how to use a socket wrench set or a pair of vice grips. My older brother won the auto shop honor his senior year in high school for rebuilding the engine in his 1967 Ford Mustang. He only had a few leftover parts at the end. I never really preferred to work on cars, myself. My passion, as it would turn out, would become rebuilding in other ways.

My job, for much of the past twenty-plus years, was to take badly damaged aircraft components and sections of heavily-damaged airframes and figure out how to remake them, piece by piece, until they were like new again. I became a tool designer, small parts manufacturer, 3D modeler, materials procurement specialist, reverse engineering master, and an artist at reading blurry blueprints from the 1960s – copies of copies where it was sometimes impossible to tell the difference between 3's and 8's and where 5's oftentimes looked like 6's and 1's were indistinguishable from 7's. It was my job to figure out how to piece the puzzle back together so that it was right, it functioned correctly, and that it was safe. If you fly commercial airplanes a good bit, chances are high that you've unknowingly bet on my ability to get all those things figured out right.

I found myself dismantling things in all parts of my life – not just at work. I bought a house with my wife, Catherine, that was begging to be ripped apart and built back up again. It was an ugly house with good bones, but there is, literally, nowhere you can go in my house where you aren't looking at something that Catherine and I haven't redone. My daughter's softball park almost died out a few years back. I've been working over the past several years with many other families in our community to rebuild it back to its glory years from thirty years ago (and we make progress every year). I own a boat now, so I know I don't even need to tell you that it automatically means I've just signed myself up for constantly rebuilding that thing every year. I've already had to reupholster my bow seat cushions, refinish the teak swim platform, and refinish its chrome trim.

Maybe it's no surprise that when I got into leadership positions at work that I looked at every team I adopted as a restoration project. I was known by my colleagues for being someone who would go in and fix an area of the business that either had not established any structure or had a structure that was broken and needed fixing. Most people who worked closely with me knew that I got bored when things were running smoothly. I'm not very good at maintaining well-built things. Whenever I got something to the point where I felt things were where they should be, I generally figured I'd leave and go to the next place that needed something redone. Otherwise, continuing to slap a new coat of the same old paint on the same thing every day just didn't get me out of bed in the morning.

Rebuilding things does require a little bit of artistry. You must make a good interpretation and not be told what all the right answers are. In fact, there are a lot of right answers. You need to figure out which of the many right answers are the best ones to make for where you are going with your build. Just the same, many wrong choices are in front of you to make. You need to be able to judge when you've made one – and if you don't catch it early, you're forced to take everything all apart and start over again. And that usually isn't very fun.

We are all going through a time right now where, almost no matter who you are, there have been many essential parts of our lives that have been completely dismantled. In a blink of an eye, all of us have been forced to make drastic changes to almost everything we used to do. Whether we like it or not, most of us have some rebuilding that we've been needing to do to get back to a new normal in this crazy new world of ours.

Mid-February 2020, I was the Director of Quality and Safety at a wholly-owned subsidiary of Delta Air Lines called Delta Flight Products, LLC (or DFP for short). We were celebrating the largest profit in our parent company's history – $1.6 billion was being doled out across the front-line employee groups as a reward for the job well done from 2019. There were parties and celebrations. Food trucks and banquet halls were overfilled with savory treats. We fired up the beer truck and had a grand old time. We did this every year for ten years running. The company had given away over $9 billion in this way over that period to its employees, who, at that point, now counted on that annual bonus.

One month later, the company was losing up to $100 million each day and I found myself on one abysmal Friday in March rounding up all of the contract employees in our building (we had about forty in the building that day) and I had to personally give them the message that, effective Monday, they were no longer going to be receiving a paycheck from us. That was one of the worst days of my career. As leaders, we had no heads-up that this was going to happen. It was a decree from the top of our division – one that I'm sure was hard to make, but it was the right decision. But it was a hard pill for us all to swallow – even harder for the many who lost their jobs that day. All anyone could do was buy those unlucky chaps a beer at the local tavern and wish them well. It was a surreal moment.

I'd been with Delta through its Chapter 11 bankruptcy days. That was a big deal, at the time, of course. But it was nothing compared to the feeling we had that day. It dawned on us that, barring intervention from on-high, every single airline in the country (if not the world) was going to be back in Chapter 11 (or even the dreaded Chapter 7 kind of bankruptcy – liquidation) within a few short months. It was such an inconceivable turn of events to go from record profits to record losses in less than a month. Covid-19, it seemed, was going to ruin us when nothing else had been able to phase us in over a decade.

Congress passed one of its bailout bills in April that included $25 billion earmarked for "loans" to the airlines. We received about $5 billion of that. One of the stipulations in the bill was that the "loan" would not have to be paid back if the company didn't lay anyone off or cut pay for any direct employees (this didn't apply to contractors, unfortunately). So none of us full-timers were laid off. And nobody took a pay cut. Instead, we all took cuts in the number of hours per week that we could get paid for. As always, every law has a creative lawyer on the other end looking for loopholes. Ours found one. If you think that translated into us only working 30 hours per week and going fishing for the other 10, that's not exactly what I said. It wasn't technically a pay cut. But it basically was. And we all, for the most part, understood. In fact, I had many of my team come to me and offer to voluntarily slash their pay and keep working full time. Everyone knew what the stakes were. We were back in that familiar "survival mode" I knew well from earlier in my career.

We all knew this was nobody's fault. We knew it was going to be a rough few months or perhaps quarters – or maybe even a few rocky years lay ahead of us. It wasn't the time to mail it in and reduce the effort we were putting into our jobs. Those of us who didn't sign up for voluntary leaves of absence (LOA) were left to run one of the most hellish skeleton crew efforts ever conceived in aviation history. No union strike ever produced so much shifting in labor roles. I did everything from driving a box truck to running logistics, to being converted to Director of Production. Hell, I even programmed and ran the old ply-cutter over at Tech Ops for a few weeks (and I must say that I had that machine humming along like never before).

The FAA Manufacturing Inspection District Office (MIDO) Aviation Safety Inspector that oversaw our production line would call me every couple of weeks to check in on me. The first time he called me, he asked how we were holding up. I said we were doing fine. Just riding it all out. Still showing up to work every day, but we had enough hands-on deck and everything was under control. The second time he called me, I told him we'd completely shut down production of aircraft parts and we were now manufacturing PPE for local hospitals, and that half or more of our staff was on LOA. The next time he called, I didn't even bother to call him back. We'd either lost every contract we had orders for or we were delayed indefinitely – one of the two. There wasn't even a point in having FAA oversight. We weren't even thinking of manufacturing anything for an aircraft anytime soon.

But don't be fooled into thinking that we were not busy. In fact, I never had a period of time that lasted as long as it did where I felt absolutely whipped every evening when I got home. I worked from 6:15 am to 8:00 pm on most days, Monday through Friday. And I got paid 25% less for that work than I did the previous year when I was working 7:30 to 5:30. Hourly reduction? Yeah, right!

We were scratching the bottom of the barrel on just about any and every idea we could come up with to save us from hemorrhaging money, somehow make ourselves some new money, or help the Covid-19 relief effort in some way in the community. We had to completely pivot on a dime and figure out any way possible to reinvent ourselves to be useful. We had to rebuild our company into something else to get us through.

One of our engineering managers, Mitch Rife, brought in an idea from a colleague of his to work with the Global Center for Medical Innovation (GCMI – an affiliate of my alma mater, Georgia Tech) to develop and mass-produce medical-grade face shields out of materials commonly available on the open market. Many of the traditional materials had completely dried up in the United States since everyone was trying to make the same things that everyone in the United States all of a sudden needed that had previously only been made everywhere in the world except right here at home.

We scoured the supply chain network for thicker tooling grade PET, polycarbonate sheet, Velcro, and adhesive-backed polyethylene foam. We ran our waterjet two shifts a day every day on that polycarbonate sheet material until it broke. Then we'd rebuild the heads, run it into the ground again, and rinse and repeat that process for the better part of the next month until we could buy enough time to get our injection molding supplier in Minnesota online to mass-produce the same parts from bead plastics. Nick Salinski, our young waterjet operator, whose family had a couple of nurses on the front lines, worked around the clock to keep the nozzles free and clear and rebuilt that machine so many times I lost count. He shoveled so much garnet sludge out of that waterjet when we finally cut off that machine that we could have turned the back parking lot into a beach.

The PET sheet that our Supply Chain Director, Mike Pechacek, found was a heavy grade. It was too heavy for most manufacturers who were making these shields at the time, so nobody wanted it. I bought over 5 tons of it. Each spool weighed over 650 lbs. and we needed a special fixture made to help it spin freely onto our ply-cutter. Rodney Brown, Gerald Sakala, and some of the other master mechanics in Delta's composite shop came up with one of the most bad-ass tool designs I've ever seen designed in such a short period of time to handle those massive spools. One of our DFP sheet metal technicians, Steve Barker, teamed up with them to develop a counter brake so it wouldn't spin out of control once that axle got going. All the guys were working so hard, as a team.

After two weeks of hand-cutting foam and Velcro spools and sheets, our wire shop supervisor, Paul Walley, came up with an idea to repurpose his wire stamping machine into a Velcro and foam cutting monster. It was ripping through thousands of pieces an hour. We were doing more in one hour with one technician on a machine than what was being done in a whole shift by a four-man crew. Everyone was coming up with ideas on how to think smarter, get faster, and recreate our business everywhere we looked.

I remember a contact at the VA Hospitals visiting our plant and they were so desperate to get their hands on this stuff. Our president, Rick, told me that his VA contact almost broke down into tears on the phone when he told them we could get them 20,000 units within the next couple of weeks. We made our delivery promise.

Mitch came forward with an idea to start making cloth masks, next. If you remember, that was about the time where the CDC was still saying that face masks were not helpful against the spread of the virus. We knew, already, that you couldn't get any. Delta had been trying to acquire millions of them for weeks at this point and to no avail.

So we decided to buy some industrial sewing machines and our manufacturing engineers went to work to build some clicker press dies, work instructions, and set up several sewing lines with one of Delta's product line managers. I was lucky to have a guy named Bobby Faulk on my manufacturing engineering team. Bobby had just finished the previous season with reupholstering his boat where, fortunately, he had to learn how to get really good with a sewing machine.

Several years back, the company had ordered 10,000 t-shirts that were never used because the necklines didn't fit right. These shirts were somewhere in a warehouse in middle-America and we ordered them out of storage and had them sent to DFP. An entire flatbed truckload of these cotton shirts came in and we had no idea where the heck we were going to store them all. So we sent them to the hangar. We planned to turn them all into masks.

The guys setting up the sewing lines stacked 10 shirts at a time on the clicker press, which is a big press machine where you put cookie-cutter sort of dies on top of the stack of material you want to cut and a hydraulic press arm comes down and presses the cookie-cutter dies into the pile of shirts and stamps out the patterns we wanted. Each time the press came down, it was enough to make 25 new masks. Off they went to the sewing line, where they were sewn by the army of volunteers there – anyone who could operate a Singer sewer was invited in to help out.

In a couple short weeks, we had thousands of masks available for company use for our front-line employees. It would be a few more weeks before shipments from China would come in for the millions of masks that our supply chain team had ordered. The day they arrived is right about the time when the CDC started to tell the story that masks actually *were* helpful.

If you visited any major airport during the Covid-19 lockdown periods (and most have not – since they were in lockdown), you may have seen some plexiglass shields, affectionately known as sneeze guards, on all of the Delta ticket counters and gate agent countertops. Justin Rogers' team, who was normally focused on designing cabin interior monuments, like galleys, closets, and other aircraft interior components, designed these at DFP. Our manufacturing plant cut them and packaged them up and sent them all over the world. They cost about $35 to make each one. Some of them cost us over $1,500 (each) to ship to some of the more exotic locations where we had to get them shipped overnight. I hand-delivered over half of them all in my box truck, along with loads of face shields, to the cargo headquarters, just down the street. Every day, I took a load down there, stood in line for about 30 minutes, filled out some forms, and unloaded them into a holding area to be overnighted to stations all over the network. We used UPS and FedEx to deliver to locations where we didn't have Delta cargo services. That's where we really racked up the costs to ship some of these things.

During all of these little side projects, our President, Rick Salanitri, and his head of design engineering, Russ Eubanks, were working on landing an unlikely project that was really big. The U.S. Air Force needed to find a company to design and build what they called a Negatively Pressurized Conex (NPC), which was essentially a desire to have a flying hospital that was equipped with a pressurized anteroom where doctors could be safe (while not in their hazmat suits treating Covid-19 infected patients) from a separate pressurized chamber that would house up to 28 patients. This Conex would be latched down inside the belly of a C-17 cargo transport aircraft and would make long-haul flights carrying infected troops back to major bases with adequate hospitals to treat the patients who were stationed in remote areas with little or no medical facilities.

The push to get these built was intense. The military was desperate to get these deployed into the field. The Air Force slashed a four-month contracting award process to just seven days; the delivery of the first prototype was demanded to be built in a matter of days from the contract award. UTS Systems was contracted as the primary supplier to the Air Force. They subcontracted the build of the container, itself, to a small company in Howell, Michigan, called Highland Engineering. Highland contracted us to do the detailed design work and to actually physically build the unit. It was designed and built in 13 days with DFP designers, manufacturing engineers, and Delta Air Lines mechanic labor.

Anne Carobine was the DFP project manager who oversaw the program. David Arwood and Dustin Genton pulled off a heroic mechanical design effort as I've never seen anyone do before (30 hours pay for at least three times that in actual time worked every week for months). Stephen Shaw was our manufacturing engineer that spearheaded the details on how this thing was getting put together on the floor. And an army of Delta mechanics made it all come together – many of whom were 30-plus year high-time leads who hadn't bucked a rivet in many years. A lot of them had been veterans, themselves, of the armed services, and it was personal for them to give to their fellow servicemen and women.

After the prototype got through testing, redesign efforts began and the team was pressed to deliver an actual battle-ready unit within the next couple of months. All-in, in less than 90 days, the Air Force had a completed, tested, and in-service NPC unit carrying its first load of patients from somewhere in the middle of nowhere to Ramstein Air Base in Germany to get relief from Covid-19.

The Colonel overseeing the project handed out accommodations to the team, suggested that we promote Anne, and handed Rick a folded American flag and acknowledged that this effort would have been impossible had it not been for the backs of the Delta people who came together to do something great with the resources we were able to scrounge together, somehow, in a few short weeks. A project of this magnitude would normally have its prototype delivered in a full year. In less than one year, to date, Delta has delivered no less than 25 completed units to their customer. The product works, it's safe, and it is a testament to the ability of a company to regroup, rebuild, and reinvent itself overnight.

In October of 2020, I have to admit it – I got to the point where I was just flat burned out. I was out of gas. It hadn't just been that last year that drained my tank. I had been a part of ongoing rebuilding / new building projects already over the past two decades. The post 9/11 and the subsequent bankruptcy was the first rebuild job that I participated in. Then, we merged with another giant airline (Northwest) and had to build a new combined company together, which was quite a task.

As a direct result of our emergence and growth within our merged company, I took on the task to rebuild the cabin operations engineering support team to further help bring premerger Delta and premerger Northwest worlds together. Then I went on to rebuild the 24-hour support engineering structure in Atlanta to funnel all subject matter support into one single group. Then I left to build a new company at DFP. While that was going on, Delta went ahead and rebuilt its hangar and the support offices on the second floor (a massive undertaking that, coincidentally, undid the build-out that I had just done in the Liaison area just a couple years prior). We even rebuilt DFP a couple times between when we opened up and before Covid-19 hit us. And now we were rebuilding, again.

I was spent. It was the right time for me to move on and move toward the next phase of my life. And we had plenty of great people who could continue to have the right energy to carry the torch as well as young leaders ready to step into the shoes of the 17,000 of us that decided to flip to the next chapter. I feel good about what I left behind and know that I left it in the capable hands of some great people. And now that I've had half a year to recharge my batteries a bit while I've started my next adventure, I'm ready to start building, again.

This is a microcosm of where we are in the United States, right now. Tens of millions of people are trying to figure out how to rebuild, yet again. How we go forward when everything goes back to some new state of "normal" isn't going to be straightforward. Reinventing ourselves is going to be tough. It'll be frustrating. It'll be hard. And it will be relentless work.

We've gone through what I hope will be the worst set of events that we'll have to deal with, as a country (heck, globally, for that matter) in the past year. Some of us have lost loved ones. Many have lost jobs. Businesses have gone under. We've been stuck at home – many of us haven't seen the inside of a gym in months. Millions of us have started completely over with new jobs (I'm one of those people), locating to new cities, and we're figuring out how to use new technologies we didn't even know existed twelve months ago. And now we can't live without them.

We'll talk about how to overcome, or at least deal with, all these things above, in this book. The bad news is that there's no easy fix for us to get to where we're going. The good news is that we've gone through all these things before, and that's going to help remind us how to deal with them, again.

It's time to shake off the rust and learn how to get back on our feet again. Buckle up, as everything is about to go back to real life, again. We'll rise out of the ashes and become the Phoenix. And we'll do it together.

Let's begin…

www.ingramcontent.com/pod-product-compliance
Lightning Source LLC
LaVergne TN
LVHW091736040425
807753LV00004B/286